A BLACK JOURNEY IN TECH

DWIGHT D. JONES SR

Copyright © 2022 by Dwight D. Jones Sr

All rights reserved. No part of this publication may be reproduced, distributed, or transmitted in any form or by any means, including photocopying, recording, or other electronic or mechanical methods, without the prior written permission of the publisher, except in the case of brief quotations embodied in critical reviews and certain other noncommercial uses permitted by copyright law.

Book Design by HMDpublishing

For My Family!
To my wife, children, grandchildren, nieces, nephews, extended family, and cousins everywhere! ......

CONTENTS

INTRODUCTION 5
1. A BLACK JOURNEY IN TECH 8
2. COUSINS 21
3. MY STORY – THE EARLY YEARS 32
4. NEVER GIVE UP! 60
5. SUPERSTARS AND HEROES: BLACK
   PEOPLE IN TECHNOLOGY! 71
6. OBSTACLES AND OPPORTUNITIES 82
7. UNDERSTANDING CHANGE 96
8. DWIGHTISMS 109
9. THE LITTLE DAD THAT COULD (WHAT ARE THE ODDS!) . 122
10. GRATITUDE! 132
11. INNOVATION AND THE FALSE NARRATIVE 140
12. HELP NEEDED 143
13. MORE WORK TO BE DONE! 151

EPILOGUE 157
RESOURCES 158

INTRODUCTION

Introduction (From humble beginnings)

May I ask you something? What kind of life would you like for yourself? If you're anything like me: maybe, you grew up with a lot of siblings; often teased for my extra pounds and thick glasses; felt like a nobody for most of my life; it was hard to even imagine a better life for myself. My high school guidance counsellor even told me that I would be dead or in jail by twenty-one. I felt like my little light was the last flicker of a cigarette butt that she used her pumps to snuff out. But I believe, in my heart of hearts, that the information I will share with you between these pages, can completely change the trajectory of your life, like it did mine.

Are you ready for an adventure in the land of tech? If so, you're on the right train. I am ready when you are.

Let's go!

Hello everyone! My name is Dwight Jones and, believe it or not, I have been a technology professional for more than thirty-six years. I come from humble beginnings, and I'm sure there was not much of a plan for my life. I was the eighth, and youngest, child of my mother's children, a Grady Baby (which is a badge of honor for Atlanta natives) as well as a latchkey kid.

As a young man, I was a ship without a rudder, sail, or compass. I felt invisible and unremarkable, destined for last place among my family and peers. I always got the drumstick while my siblings (who were so much older than me) munched on breasts and thighs.

We lived in Perry Homes, a housing project in Atlanta. My dad did well enough in his trucking business that, by the time I was born, he was able to move the family (all ten of us) to our first real home, a two- bedroom, "shotgun" house on Old Know Drive near the infamous Bankhead Highway in northwest Atlanta.

When I was five, we moved to a five-bedroom home on the southwest side of the city, in an upper middle class, Black neighborhood. We were surrounded by Black excellence: PhDs, educators, postal workers, clergy, businessmen, professional athletes, and politicians. I was raised with their children, but my status seemed to be last in those circles, too.

But somewhere along the way, my paradigm changed.

Today I am a Principal Program Manager for Microsoft Corporation, a top performer with a strong technical, program and service management background. I have designed, managed, and supported server, network, and telecommunication systems for companies such as WH Smith, Waterstones Booksellers, Bank of America, Norfolk Southern Railway and BellSouth Internet Services. For nineteen years, I have been a Microsoft employee. What a ride it's been!

I welcome you to take this ride with me.

Chapter 1: A BLACK JOURNEY IN TECH

At Microsoft, I started in 2003 as a network engineer with MSN Global Network Services (now Azure), then took a customer-facing role as a Senior Engagement Manager for Microsoft TV, bringing AT&T (U-verse) to market. Later I became a Senior Service Engineering Manager in Microsoft Digital (formerly Microsoft IT), where, for thirteen years, I supported many Microsoft enterprise technologies including: Network Access Protection, IPsec, Radius, Virtual Private Networking and Certificate Services.

In March 2014, I began working with Employee Experience, continuing as a Senior Service Engineering Manager where I led Service Management, tier 3 engineering support, Livesite and Problem Management processes for o365 technologies: Skype for Business, Microsoft Teams, SharePoint, and Exchange for Microsoft's internal users globally.

In 2020, I was promoted to Principal Program Manager spearheading the Employee Experience team responsible for proving to the world that Microsoft could support government programs safely and securely in the Azure Government Cloud.

Over the expanse of my career, I have received numerous commendations for technical excellence and leadership.

Here are a few that I am most proud of:

2002 I received a plaque for Outstanding Job Performance and a Certificate of Excellence from BellSouth Internet Services. I received industry recognition for deploying the first global Network Automation tool at Microsoft by Opsware. At the time it was True Control. It later became HP Network Automation.

I am a Microsoft Gold Star Award recipient which is reserved for top talent. I am also a five-time Deliver IT and 7-time IT Excellence award recipient. However, I am most proud to be the CIO Award Recipient. This was called the "Tony Award" as it was named after our CIO at the time Tony Scott. This was the highest individual Microsoft IT Honor. What made winning this award so special is that my peers voted for me to receive this high honor.

Former Microsoft IT CIO Jim Dubois presenting me with the CIO Award (2013)

Why am I telling you all this? Because I truly believe my background will inspire you to reach higher than you've ever imagined you could. I want you to understand that with dedicated work and faith you can build an impressive body of experience that you can be proud of!

But here's the problem: there is an underrepresentation of Black people in technology also referred to as the Digital Divide. I want to help close this egregious gap, which I think is due, in part, to the contributions of Black people in tech being buried by the lies and misrepresentations that have followed our culture ever since we set foot on these complicated shores.

The truth is my people have always contributed to technical advancement but since this fact has been overlooked, many of my people don't see themselves in technology, and assume that those roles are not for them. This means far too many Black people are missing out on opportunities that working in tech can provide.

Did you know that the VOIP technology that allows us to meet in Zoom or Teams calls, the Electret microphone in your computer and mobile device, and the first digital cell phone were contributions made by Black inventors? True stories like these (including my own) could be the flicker to light a flame beneath you and propel you to success in technology.

In my case, God changed my perspective and blessed me with an outstanding career. I want to share my story with you, especially if you are interested in technology. I want to encourage and remind you that our God is no respecter of persons. If He can move mountains for me, He will do the same for you. I want you to know that inside of you is an untapped reservoir of talent and skills. Don't accept the narrative that technologists are from *other* cultures. Even if you feel marginalized and untethered, you CAN be successful in technology! Believe this when you feel most isolated and alone. You are capable of bridging the digital divide.

My journey down the long, winding road of technology began in 1986 on my father's birthday, March 3rd. I was an assistant third-shift computer operator, making seven dollars an hour. This career choice seemed small at the time but has opened countless doors for me. I am so grateful for it. This life-altering decision took me from humble beginnings to a career that has made me a millionaire.

More importantly, this career has taken me from the low bar set for my existence to leading highly complex projects and travelling the globe for one of the top technology companies in the world. I feel like a pioneer, lifted up by my parents and building a legacy for others like me. My journey has not been easy; there were bumps and setbacks along the way, but yes, it was worth it.

My wife and four of my six children are all Microsoft full-time employees. When I coach and mentor folks, I tell them there is no ceiling in technology. There is space for us all.

A quick look back

When I was a child, I felt lots of uncertainty about the future. When anyone asked me what I wanted to do when I grew up, I would shrug my chubby shoulders or lower my eyes behind my thick glasses and say, "I don't know." There just didn't seem to be a lot of options for me.

In high school, my cluelessness was masked by my involvement in sports and Army ROTC (Reserve Officers' Training Corp). These gave me structure, teammates, and goals. Everyone on my football team dreamed of winning a college scholarship, playing college football, and making it to the pros.

I grew up in the era of Michael Jordan and Dominique Wilkins. I actually went to school with Dominique's brothers and the Browner's, where Ross (Bengals), Joey (Vikings) and Keith (49ers) all made it to the NFL. So, we walked the halls beside athletes who actually made it to the top of their professions, and we thought we could get there too.

But the reality was that most of us were closer to the character in the movie *Rudy* where a college athlete spent years practicing, sweating, and struggling, only to play in ONE game. That was the extent of his career.

My teammates and I yearned to fit in, to play ball and be filthy rich adults living in Buckhead, buying our mothers houses with two kitchens and a glistening pool in the backyard. But deep inside, we knew our chances were slim to none.

Now I am not saying that you cannot dream and believe and have faith, but you must understand that you will be *one in a million* if you're aiming to enter the Glory Land of professional sports.

I happen to know one of those one in a million, Dwight Howard. He was number 1 in the NBA draft in 2004, eighteen years of age and right out of high school. This future Hall of Famer has spent 18 years in the NBA, and he's still going strong. He just earned 10th place all-time for rebounds in the NBA. I've watched him grow into a great young man, truly a needle in a haystack crowded with dreamers. His parents are my amazing, fellow prayer warriors and they've always reached out to support children in our community. I am a huge fan of the Howards.

I am a life-long Dwight Howard fan. Whenever he comes to Portland, I make the 2.5-hour drive from Seattle to reconnect.

If you are in middle school, high school or college and have no idea what you want to do with your life, this book is for you. If you're an inmate, confused and troubled, this is your book. Just lost your job or in desperate need of a career change? Your book is in your hands.

Maybe you're an immigrant, struggling to learn English, in search of prosperity and the security that technology brings. Maybe you've retired from one career or you're just out of the military.

I am telling you that you can find purpose and a great life in technology. It provided me an avenue that stretched further than my lack, my uncertainty, and my bad credit score, and put me in a place of prosperity. I did not get drafted number 1 in the NBA or in the NFL, but in 2003, I plugged into a company called Microsoft and I've been able to provide for my family to the degree I've never dreamed possible. I live, work, and learn beside millionaires, all because of my skills, passion, faith, and perseverance.

Dilemma by Design (The Boom that Busted Black Folk)

I live in the city of Bellevue, Washington very close to Redmond, which is Microsoft's corporate headquarters. Redmond is a suburb, just across Interstate 90, and a twelve-minute drive from Seattle. It started as farmland but today Redmond is a place of great wealth.

In Medina, which is a suburb of Bellevue, there are more billionaires per capita than anywhere else in the United States. Yes, even more than Beverly Hills. They are building condos on top of condos on the daily. Microsoft has torn down its main campus and is building the campus of the future. They've even constructed a rail line to connect Redmond to Seattle.

Why are they doing this? Because of the opportunities in technology! This is not just happening for Microsoft; other companies have moved to the Pacific Northwest, like Amazon, Google, and Space X.

So, I have a question for you. Instead of trying to be the next Dwight Howard, Lebron James, Jay-Z or Beyonce, why not consider hitching your wagon to technology? Start building up your faith muscles so that you have the courage to leave your comfort zone and move to a place where everyone at the grocery store is probably a millionaire. Makes sense? Good! Keep reading.

Microsoft has had two great booming eras. The first was when Bill Gates founded the company and was its CEO. That was when Microsoft made more millionaires than any company in history.

When I first joined the company, this became a familiar scene: someone would point to an admin or receptionist and say, "she is worth millions." I couldn't believe it! Or someone would tell me a story about how they shrink-wrapped software, literally put CDs or disks in a box, *and became rich as they grew with the company.* As a matter of fact, one of the benefits of being a Microsoft employee is the opportunity to buy life insurance at ten times or more of your salary. If you make $100k per year, you have just boosted your value to your first million. If you buy a house in a place like Redmond, more than likely that house will be valued at a million dollars. That's two million right there. The first Microsoft Boom made Redmond an international city. There are people here from all over the world amassing great wealth and prosperity.

But Black people largely missed this boom and its accompanying prosperity. This is very vexing to me because I know the opportunities are here and so is the money. Why has every culture taken root and flourished except my own? After all Redmond, Bellevue and the surrounding cities are in *Martin Luther King County for goodness sakes*! Why, in such an international place, is the Black population less than two percent, and in the entire state, less than four percent? Why, even though Blacks at Microsoft (BAM) is the oldest Employee Resource Group (ERG) in Microsoft, created thirty-one years ago to help Black people grow as a community inside of the company, have Black people not prospered at the same rate as other races? I think I know part of the answer.

During the time that Microsoft was experiencing the first boom, Seattle was going through a huge red-lining and gentrification effort designed to systematically displace Black folks. Black people in the Central District in Seattle (that was more than seventy-three percent Black) were targeted for removal. Not one African American received an FHA loan for housing in a five-year period in that part of Seattle. In cities like Redmond and Bellevue, it was written in the covenants and bylaws that you could not sell housing to a Black person. This made it pretty much impossible for us to establish roots in the community that I call home. This is documented in the PBS special that you can watch on YouTube titled: On the Brink | PBS.

Seattle Neighborhoods with Restrictive Covenants

Seattle
Alki
Ballard
Beacon Hill
Bitter Lake
Blue Ridge
Broadmoor
Bryant
Capitol Hill
Central District
Duwamish
Eastlake
Greenlake
Greenwood
Haller Lake
Hawthorne Hills
Lake City
Lakeridge Laurelhurst
Loyal Heights
Madrona
Magnolia
Maple Leaf
Matthews Beach
Montlake
Olympic Hills
North Beach/Blue Ridge
North College Park
Northgate
Pinehurst
Queen Anne
Queen Anne Lower
Queen Anne North
Rainier Valley Ravenna
Sandpoint
Sheridan Beach
Vashon Island
Victory Heights
View Ridge
Wedgewood
West Seattle/High Point
Windermere

Eastside
Ames Lake
Arrowhead Point
Bellevue
Clyde Hill
Inglewood
Juanita
Kirkland
Lake Alice
Lake Sammamish
Mercer Island
North Bend
Redmond
Sammamish

North King Co.
Ballinger (Shoreline)
Briarcrest (Shoreline)
Echo Lake (Shoreline)
Hamlin Park (Shoreline)
Hillwood (Shoreline)
Innis Arden (Shoreline)
Kenmore
Lake Forest Park
North City (Shoreline)
Richmond Beach (Shoreline)
Richmond Highlands (Shoreline)
Ridgecrest (Shoreline)
Westminster Triangle (Shoreline)

South King Co.
Arbor Heights
Arroyo Heights
Auburn
White Center
Boulevard Park
Maple Valley
McMicken Heights
Normandy Park
Redondo
Renton

4. No person or persons of Asiatic, African or Negro blood, lineage or extraction shall be permitted to occupy a portion of said property, or any building thereon; except, domestic servant or servants may be actually and in good faith employed by white occupants of such premises.

in King County, State of Washington, the particular description of the lands and additions to which the instrument applies is contained in and follows the several signatures of the makers of this instrument. The parties hereto signing and executing this instrument and the several like instruments relating to their several properties in said district, hereby mutually covenant, promise and agree each with the others, and for their respective heirs and assigns that no part of the lands owned by them as described following their signatures to this instrument shall ever be used or occupied by or sold, conveyed, leased rented or given to negroes or any person or persons of the negro blood.

> the Rainier Valley by Seattle's lending institutions. Data to be presented in this study shows a total redlining of major portions of the Central Area and complete redlining of the Rainier Valley.
>
> According to public records:
>
> 1. No conventional or FHA loans were granted in the last five years in large parts of the Central Area by nearly all banks except to speculators or investors.
>
> 2. Only FHA insured loans through mortgage companies are available to Central Area and Rainier Valley residents -- at higher costs.
>
> 3. The foreclosure rate by the major mortgage companies active in the redlined areas is up to eight times that of most banks.

1970
Black Population in Central District

73%

2014
Black Population in Central District

18%

Fortunately, by the year 2000, most of the inequities were corrected, but the damage had been done. I don't believe Black people will ever be able to regain that lost prosperity. They definitely missed the housing boom where their two hundred-thousand-dollar home could easily be worth two million today. But they were forced out and had to sell their homes for far less than the current value. The dye has been cast, and there is just no way to recover from this. The gulf caused by the housing crisis and the social/economic divide in Seattle is second only to the gulf between hell and heaven. Most blue-collar workers, the backbone of our society, can't afford to live here. Atlanta beware!

Today, Microsoft and other tech companies, have another pressing challenge: how to attract and retain talent from the Black community. How do I know this is a major hurdle? Not only have I been the chairperson for several of the Black at Microsoft Chapters (BAM) but I'm also presently a co-lead of the Microsoft Digital BAM community.

But there is hope for the future. Under Satya Nadella, Microsoft is on a second boom even greater than the first. I have watched our stock value move from the $30s per share to nearly $350 per share. The company is growing. The surrounding area is expanding and building for the future. Hear me when I say, now is the time to become a technologist!

Microsoft has vowed to use its power and influence to make the world a better place. Rebuilding the campus while working to become carbon neutral is one example. Through our *Give Campaign*, Microsoft was the first company to exceed a billion dollars donated to charity. The company also provides legal support to improve the criminal justice system and to help end systemic racism.

Today the senior leadership team acknowledges the abysmal lag in hiring members of the Black and Hispanic community, and they have responded by putting forth specific goals to improve hiring and career pathways for Black employees.

So, my question for you: are you ready to ride into the land of possibility? I'm ready to guide you there. I'll share the story of a lost young man who had no idea what he wanted to be when he grew up. Today he's a man who lays a solid path for his family. Today he's me.

I pray your mind is as open as a parachute, and that you know you can achieve great things too! I think you'll enjoy meeting me on these pages and feel encouraged and empowered to start your own journey. You'll have to take some calculated risks and burn the midnight oil learning what you need to know to get where you want to go, but that's okay; it's all part of the game. Technical jobs are not going away, and if you are willing to claim your piece of the pie, I promise that you'll find a seat at the table.

Chapter 2:
COUSINS

MY NAME IS DWIGHT JONES, AND I THINK WE ARE COUSINS!

Let's take a journey and find out how!

1. My present day life
2. Known U.S. (African American) history
3. Let's look back a bit further

I think we are cousins, and I can prove it to you by the end of this chapter. I'll share a little bit about myself and my family and then take a look back at my ancestry. I want to connect with you personally because I think I can prove we're related.

I was born in Atlanta, Georgia at Grady Memorial Hospital on November 3rd, 1965, to Joe (42) and Gertrude Jones (40). My 96-year-old mother and I talk almost every day. I am a huge, huge mama's boy. ☺ Mama's eighth and favorite child. I am so blessed to be beloved by her and my sisters and brothers: Gwendolyn, Betty, Joe III, Taft, Deborah, Phillip and Phyllis, and my big extended family, all based in the A-T-L.

*Left Taft, Gwen, Betty, Middle Joe III, Phyllis, Mother Right me, Deborah, Phillip
Figure 2 Betty, Phyllis, Mother Gertrude, Taft, Me, Joe III*

My mother worked the 3pm–11pm shift as a nurse's assistant at Grady Memorial Hospital twelfth floor, D Unit (12-D) for 20 years. She spent her career giving such tender love to severely high risk, premature babies. She was amazing at her work and is a phenomenal mother.

My father, Joe Jones, Jr., was born on March 3, 1923, in Milledgeville, Ga., a tiny town outside of Atlanta that used to have an unsavory reputation as the home of an insane asylum.

My dad was a WWII vet who fought to liberate France as part of the US Army's Red Ball Express. Later in his short life, he became a businessman and pretty much an icon to his children. His fight for the right to provide for us was highly publicized.

He had his own trucking company, and he wanted to expand so he could transport goods across the United States, but to do this, he needed the Interstate Commerce Commission (ICC) to grant him a license. Because he was Black, he was denied the license and the story ("A Negro is Denied His 7th Appeal for the ICC License") wound up in national newspapers. His plight even wound up being featured on Atlanta's WSB Channel 2 News.

But thank goodness, Joe Jones Jr. had no quit in his blood. He took his fight to the White House steps where he sat with his little protest sign until he got to meet with President Lyndon Johnson and received that license!

My father was on the road most of the time and sadly, he died of lung cancer when I was twelve. I was devastated. I always yearned to be by his side. After he got sick, he spent more time at home and with me. He took me fishing and signed me up to play baseball with the Cascade Youth Organization major league Reds. He even let me rub his bald head and push him around a bit, even though he had lost so much weight and was weak from the chemo. I was finally getting the time with my father that I had been praying for then, with one phone call, it all got ripped away.

My sister Deborah was running through the house crying an uncontrollable, soul wrenching cry. "Daddy is gone! Daddy is gone!" We all joined in the tearful cry, "Daddy is gone!"

I learned that there is no coming back from this kind of pain. My life was immediately and permanently disrupted by an unplanned change, and I'll spend the rest of my days trying to adapt to this unalterable fact: I will never talk to my hero again.

My grandfather, Joseph Codear Jones (Joe Jones Sr.), was born a slave, and as a matter of fact, we received the name *Jones* from the Jones plantation in Staunton, Virginia. I consider myself very blessed to have been on the receiving end of this man's warmth and affection. I was privileged to know him while he was alive.

One of my earliest memories centered around the sense of wholeness, trust, and security I felt riding in a car between him and my father. I only had a couple of visits with my grandfather, but I remember them very well.

Joseph Jones had a small weather beaten, wood-planked house that you could see clean under because it stood on cylinder bricks. Vegetables and watermelon grew in his yard. There was no paved driveway. You turned off the road onto Georgia red clay, and a few bumps later, you were in front of the house.

He worked in a security booth for a cement company, and I can remember my dad driving me to visit him at his job, and while we were in town, we'd also spend time with my lovely half-sister Hazel whom I love dearly. She still lives in Milledgeville to this day.

I remember falling asleep on my grandfather's lap as my father drove him to meet the family in Atlanta. I remember his hand guiding me by the back of my head or on my shoulders as I stood by the car after the long drive from Milledgeville to Atlanta. My grandfather passed in 1971 and is buried in the slave section of that city's historic cemetery.

The oldest I can go back in my own US family history is to my great grandparents. My great grandfather fought in the Spanish American war and his wife was a Cherokee Indian. Quite unfortunately, we do not know their names, but we do know that they were both massacred in the Virginia persecution of slaves forcing my grandfather to flee to the South.

What a story, right! Now you see what I mean when I say I stand on the shoulders of giants. The lessons I've learned from the lives of my ancestors inspires me to push hard for a better future for me and my loved ones and reminds me that I was born of strength, pride, resilience, and fortitude.

My dad proudly standing by one of his truck   *Granddaddy making the papers in Milledgeville*

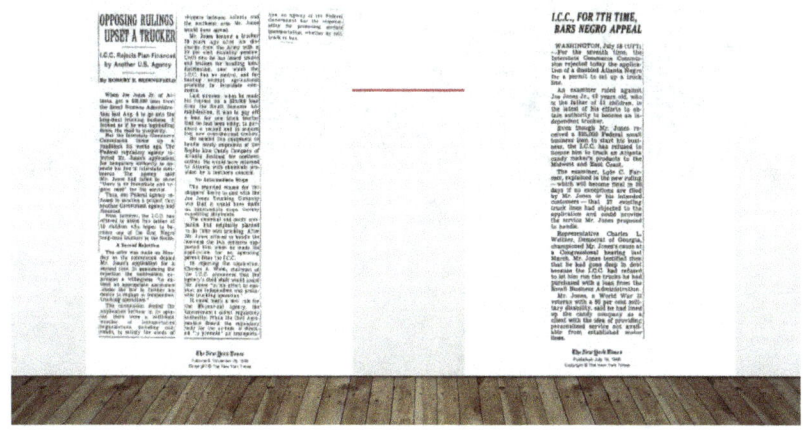

My father's battle for the I.C.C. license was often in the media.

I met my wife Yolanda in my junior year of high school. She went to Frederick Douglass High school, and I attended Benjamin E. Mays High school on the other side of town. Shout out to the class of 83!

We started dating in August of 1983, right before she went off to Xavier University in New Orleans. I went to Georgia State University.

Yolanda and I dated throughout college and got married on July 11, 1987. We've been married for thirty-five years and are the parents of six uniquely amazing children. Seven if you include my son in law. I have three beautiful granddaughters and one handsomely debonair grandson. I expect that my children and grandchildren will bring our family's brilliance, humor, and zaniness into the next generation.

My wife, children and grandchildren

Me, Yolanda, and the grands in our natural state!

March 2022 marks my thirty-sixth year as a technical professional. I'm proud to say that I've worked, learned, and contributed to the success of many companies across several industries.

I love driving complex technical initiatives and being at the helm of high-performing teams to take on the toughest challenges and delivering a best-in-class result.

I spent many rewarding years as a Service Engineering Manager supporting Microsoft's internal users globally.

Now let's pivot away from my U.S. family's history so I can say what an awesome tool DNA testing has become. It has allowed us to fill in pieces of our life puzzles that we did not even know were missing. Surprise! I share lineage with French royalty! I share the paternal ancestry with King Louis XVI. I am a distinguished member of the house of Bourbon kings, founded by my apparent ancestor King Henry IV. More importantly, I share DNA with people from just about every inhabitable place on earth. According to my DNA map, the only places that I did not inherit DNA from are Greenland, Central Europe, and Australia.

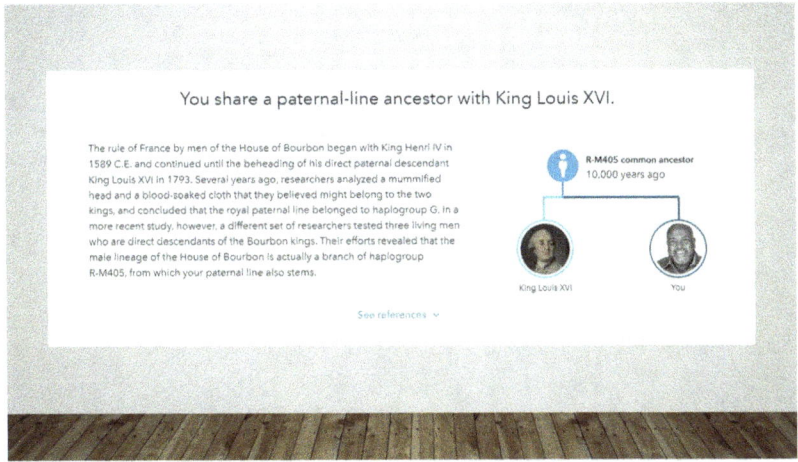

My DNA map shows my Irish, French, German, Scandinavian, West Africa, Central & Southern Africa, Iberian, Eastern European, Native American, Italian, Balkan, Southeast Asian, Ashkenazi Jewish and Finnish ancestry. I also have distant relatives from Great Britain. I am actually 23% European. Who knew! This explains my lifelong love of all people and my burning desire to build relationships. Knowing that I am connected with so many people from all across the world makes me happy. My question to you is does my DNA ancestry cross paths with yours? If yes, then I think we are cousins! I will be waiting for my invitation to our next family reunion. ☺

Rank	Ancestry	Number of DNA Relatives with ancestry
1	British & Irish	740
2	French & German	565
3	Scandinavian	490
4	West African	240
5	Central & South African	175
6	Iberian	135
7	Eastern European	90
8	Native American	60
9	Italian	45
10	Balkan	30
11	Southeast Asian	25
12	Ashkenazi Jewish	15
13	Finnish	5

How does an African American man, grandson of a slave, last of eight children, college dropout and father of six, rise from a life of odds stacked against him to become a respected technology professional at one of the top technology companies in the world? Well, that's the story I'm about to share with you. Trust me, I won't be tooting my own horn; sharing my story will be a signpost announcing: **this way to beat the odds!**

I hope that you, dear cousin, know that where you are today does not dictate what or where you will be in the future. Life is a gift. A precious journey, but it's really up to each one of us to press toward our dreams or allow life's waves to overwhelm and carry us to the Land of Wherever.

I think of the passage in the Bible where Jesus was walking on the water and Peter, his disciple, asked to join him. Jesus said, "Come." And Peter walked on the water under the same power and authority of the Master. As long as his eyes were on Jesus, Peter was able to do the impossible, but when his mind took over, and he looked at the waves and realized he was standing on top of deep water in the midst of a storm, he began to sink.

This parable explains how I got from there to here. Life has always felt big, but I have a belief system. I know that if God be for me, then who can be against me? I believe that my Heavenly Father created the universe, and the earth is His. If He loves me, and He put me here, He will make a way for me. I just have to keep my eyes on Him.

I can identify with Peter. I was born into water over my head, and it seemed as I grew older, the water only got deeper. But guess what? It doesn't matter how scary the water is if you keep your eyes on the Master of the seas. God created the water *and* me.

In my spirit, I can hear the song that has comforted earthly souls all over the world, "Love lifted me. When nothing else could help, love lifted me!"

Chapter 3:
MY STORY – THE EARLY YEARS

This life has always felt too hard for me, and so have my goals. I never fit the mold or was anyone's first choice. I was an overweight kid with coke bottle glasses and two silver teeth in the front of my mouth. The real ones were knocked out playing a game I created called Charlie-Chaplin-From-The-Chorus-Risers. Yikes! The object was to face plant without catching yourself like Charlie did in the movies, only you did this from each level of the chorus risers. Yay–I won! Which left me with two front teeth that were silver way before rappers made grills fashionable.

6th grade (I think!)

Let's say I stood out in a crowd, but not in a good way. Those silver caps were supposed to be temporary, but I got my first job in tech and married with those headlights still on high beam.

Marrying at twenty-one, six children by age thirty-one, poor credit, and of course, never enough money, were constant obstacles. I had to find something bigger than myself, bigger than my circumstances, to focus on. Thank goodness I found my faith in Jesus Christ.

My family dynamic was very interesting. We were Christian and God-fearing, with a strong military heritage, however, we were not overboard or overzealous. We are a blended and complicated clan. I don't even know all the dynamics of my own family. All I am certain of is that we love each other, and through that love and connectedness, we care for each other infinitely.

My oldest two sisters, Gwen (deceased) and Betty, were part of my life growing up and had the last name Wyatt. The rest of us were Jones. I promise you I was nearing adulthood before I even thought to question why. It doesn't matter. They are my sisters.

From my mother and father's marriage there are six children: Joe Jones III, Taft Vincent Jones, Deborah Mary Jones Weaver (who passed away from lung cancer), Phillip Andre' Jones, Phyllis Carson Jones Churn and me. I have a younger half-sister, Cecelia Uylesses Jones and my father also had a child from before he met my mother, Hazel Payne.

My father was a World War II vet, an Army private who fought to liberate France as part of the famed all-Black unit The Red Ball Express. I have two brothers who served in Vietnam. One was a Marine, and one was in the Air Force. My brother Phillip was in the US Army. My oldest brother, Joe Jones III, volunteered for the Marines.

I was a toddler, but I still remember Joe. He would play with me and do magic tricks that made coins and key chains disappear and reappear. The dude was magical! He let me sit in his girlfriend's lap (Carmen Haley). Although I couldn't've been more than three years old, I still recall thinking what a cool brother to share his girlfriend with me. ☺

I remember there was conflict in the family when he announced that he was joining the Marines. I don't think my parents were happy with his decision because the country was at war. I remember us all crying when he was going away for bootcamp. I remember the sorrow shifting eventually to a sense of family pride and patriotism. My dad would rent these huge campers and drive the entire family to Paris Island, South Carolina to watch my brother in basic training. We drove there twice in the campers then stuffed ourselves in cars for his graduation.

One of my fondest memories was my dad and him wrestling on a pier that bordered the water. Dad said he was testing his son's hand-to-hand combat skills as the rest of us watched in panic. But we were all so proud.

My brother Joe never forgot me when he was away. The first gift that he gave me was my red and white "I am a little marine" shirt. That planted the seed! I wanted to be a marine. I wore that shirt from the time I was three until I was about seven. It was my favorite.

I can also remember my hot wheels racing car set with the yellow tracks that he bought me for Christmas. Joe has always watched over me. Even when I saw him recently on a trip to see my mother and my family, he was still doting over me. He is sixteen years older than me, and he would give me the hat off his head and buy me three more. If you see me in a picture with a hat on, it was probably from Joe.

When Joe III left us in 1968, we were nine deep in a two-bedroom, one bathroom house on 2546 Old Know Drive in northwest Atlanta. Mom and Dad had a bedroom. Phyllis and Betty shared a full-size bed. In the same room, there was a bunk bed that Deborah and I shared, even though I would always end up in her bed, either by choice or because I fell from the top bed and we'd just drift off to sleep again.

Joe, Taft, and Phillip somehow shared twin beds in what should have been a dining room. There was a living room and a kitchen and that was it.

We also shared space with my dogs Brownie and Spot. Brownie was a beautiful golden retriever with a coat the color of new pennies. She would let me hug her, and although she was a dog and lived outside, I had mad love and respect for her and spent time with her every day.

Spot was a border-collie mix. He was black and white and was about the business of keeping us safe. I don't remember this part, but I was told that he would babysit me in my walker, and would pull me back whenever I ventured over to the porch steps.

How can I remember things that happened to me when I was so small? Most people can only go as far back as five. Maybe my memory is so vivid because of the terrible seizures I used to have when I was a tiny boy. I remember one of these episodes.

My family surrounded me. I can still smell the panic. Someone sent for Mrs. Green from across the street. I can remember how

I seemed to be watching my family from behind their fear-struck bodies. I saw Mrs. Green rushing to my house to save me as I hovered over a tree (spirit-like) in my yard. I can remember my brief chuckle as she slipped on the way to the house. This beautiful brown, heavy-set lady picked up my body and squeezed me in her arms, rocking me as she prayed out loud and called on the name of Jesus. I was behind them all, watching. I remember waking in my body as she held me tight. And from that point on, I can recall most of my life before I turned five.

One day, my dad allowed me to climb into his tractor-trailer truck. I can still see my mother's anxious eyes. I learned to ride a single speed bike without training wheels at about 3 years of age; I sold watermelon for 50 cents from our yard with my brothers. Once upon a time, Taft and Joe locked me into the truck's trailer full of watermelon as a joke. I still see Phil and Robert Jr on their minibikes, speeding around the curve on Hood drive. I haven't forgotten preschool at Haugabrook's Academy and my teacher, Mrs. Haley, Carmen's mother, giving me a ride home in her sky-blue Chevy. I remember my Delta Airlines lunchbox and one evening seeing the Haley's house on fire. I remember walking around the yard with pickled pig feet in my mouth, and my sister Deborah working for Rich's downtown, taking me to ride *The Pink Pig*. I remember her buying me a white coat with blue fur and the envy spreading across my brother's face at the sight of it. I remember him throwing an orange peel in front of the camera as I posed in my new coat. I remember my cousins Cookie and Walt coming over with two beautiful white dogs. Today my memory is not as sharp, but I still remember so much from way back when.

When Taft, my second to the oldest brother, joined the Air Force and was going overseas, we all drove to Warner Robbins Air Force base and said our goodbyes at the air strip. We watched as he took off in a B-52 headed to Thailand.

Taft is the most practical of us all. He has taught me so many life lessons. One of them was in response to one of my letters which were typically, "hello, how are you? What are you going to bring me?"

I loved writing letters to my brothers when they were away in the military because they always wrote me back, even though their letters weren't always full of smiles and good cheer.

Like the time Taft penned a very serious letter to me. I was in the first or second grade. He wrote that I should not just write asking for things; that since he was far away from home, he wanted me to write to ask how HE was doing and to tell him what I was up to. I did not like the bluntness of the letter, but it taught me a lesson about empathy. I immediately understood that he was isolated and away and could not be around the family that he loved and that this was painful to him.

After that lesson, my letters were more mature. I was not focusing on what my big brother could do for me. I understood that he was serving the country during a time of war, and I became more concerned about him making it safely back home.

From there to here – Pivotal Moments:

Pivotal Moment #1: Sunday School

My mother is a proud Christian woman. She is on the Mother Board (a position of honor in the Black church, held by long-serving elders and wise women) at Greater Fair Hill Baptist Church and she also serves as a deaconess. Some of my earliest memories come from being raised in the church, a fundamental place for me as a child and for our family. The communities that I was raised in pretty much had this in common, although these groups had a lot of things (other than Christianity) in common too.

Some of these memories were about the importance my mother placed on having us dressed and ready for Sunday service. It was always a formal occasion, and you always wore your best to worship. Suit and tie, with polished shoes, was standard attire.

Mama would have her seven children (Gwen was in college) walking to church from our two-bedroom house on Old Know, raggedy on the outside, but clean on the inside. Every Saturday we were all-hands-on-deck, cleaning the entire house til it was spotless. WAOK, the local AM radio station, would be playing with the volume up high. My sister Betty would assign us our duties and ensure that execution was flawless. My mother and father did not need to supervise; we always gave Betty the respect of being the eldest. Of course, I was too young to participate, so I just watched. ☺

The route to church was simple: a left turn out of the house, a brief walk up the street, then a right onto Commercial Avenue where the rapper T.I. says you went to "get the work." We'd walk past the candy lady's house (Mrs. Clark), Luke's and the Park's house, and see plenty of people out selling and sipping. They were always polite to us when we were with my mother. "Hey Mrs. Jones. Say a prayer for me Mrs. Jones!" Then we'd turn left on Rockwood Avenue, a side street that connects Bankhead to H.E. Holmes Drive. Hightower Road to those of you with Atlanta roots.

I can remember my mother holding my hand while carrying her neatly pressed choir robe, satin green with a resplendently gold collar that formed a triangle in the front and back. My father was never with us. The only two times I can remember him being in church was one New Year's Eve when he joined my mother for a watch night service, and when he gave my sister Deborah away at her wedding.

Of course, he was there for his funeral, which was a self-fulfilled prophecy. He would always say that Pastor Jones would one day funeralize him there. Despite his absence from church, dad was always supportive of my mother and was proud of how she raised her family. In fact, he donated all the red bricks that built the church's first sanctuary that still stands today, and he was the money behind those sharp Sunday suits and Easter clothes we so proudly wore.

Trips to Kessler's (if you don't know bout this department store, you better ask somebody) and to Ms. Betty's, the seamstress, were very important to my mother.

We couldn't just *attend* church; we had to be *involved* in the church, singing in the choir, serving as ushers, stumbling through Easter speeches, baptized, and enrolled in Sunday school and vacation bible school. Even when we moved from the Bankhead area to southwest Atlanta in 1971, we continued to stay connected to our old community through the church. I have so many relationships that stemmed from this era of my life. Up until I graduated from high school, I was with my mother at church two or three times a week.

Sunday school has a learning path similar to that of the formal education system. It goes from pre-k to adults. I participated all the way up through my teen years.

When I was about four, after Sunday class, all the children would have to stand and summarize the lesson of the day. This was my favorite thing to do. I couldn't wait to expound on a perspective and share a deeper message, even at such a tender age.

To this day, I believe that God imbued me with vision and insight so that I could share messages with the congregation from a different lens. My words would always land the "amens" from the adults, and this was a gift. I can remember Sister Geraldine Jones pulling me aside and saying, "Dwight, God has great things planned for you." I'd hear similar affirmations from Deacons Stewart and Holiday.

My all-time favorite class was my mother's. She and Deaconess Doris Dudley taught a young adult class that brought me such pleasure. Those ladies poured their hearts into teaching us the sacred word of God. I felt so close to her then, as she shared with me what was most precious to her, the Gospel. To this day, my mother and I discuss Scripture in every conversation. She truly laid the love of the Lord at the foundation of my life.

Pivotal Moment #2: Mrs. Sewell's 6th grade class

It was, as they say, the best of times and the worst of times. I was five years old when my family moved from a two-bedroom home near Bankhead into a five bedroom, three level house in southwest Atlanta. We finally lived in a house that was just as nice on the outside as it was on the inside. It was a mansion compared to our previous home, although most of us still had to share bedrooms.

Back to being five: I remember this year so vividly because up to that point, I had been in my mother's constant care. The only exception was a brief time I'd attended Haugabrook's Academy where Mrs. Haley was my pre-school teacher. I don't remember this lasting more than a few weeks or maybe a month, and it seemed to start just as quickly as it ended. But I do remember my disdain for going to kindergarten and my first day at West Manor Elementary. I did not want to leave my mother's side and I definitely expressed my displeasure. Until I got to my kindergarten class, and it was cool.

Mrs. Bell, my kindergarten teacher, was a blast! We got to eat, color with crayons, take naps and play. It was my introduction to Legos and classmates, some of whom are still my friends on Facebook. I was only there for half days, but it didn't take long for me to prove that I was mature enough to handle being outside of Mama's watchful eye.

That was until she carried me with her on an interview for WHAT'S THIS? a job!

My five-year old brain could not wrap itself around her not being at home. She did not have to be with me all the time, but I needed to know that she was in the next room, there when I needed her. Mother was always preparing our meals for the day, or keeping our much bigger home clean, on the phone with sister so and so, or reading her bible. I was young but already ingrained in the Archie Bunker/George Jefferson traditions of Mama at home, Daddy at work. My father's plan was to be the provider and for his wife to stay home and take care of the house and family. Well, reality changed that. My father could not always pay the bills, and my mother was determined to go to work.

Now, I remember the interview, and I will not go into all the details, but as the actors Will Ferrell and John C. Reilly taught us in the movie *Stepbrothers*, it's not a good idea to double up for interviews. I was there to crash the party. I gave the stink eye, the side eye, the mean mug, and the outburst, all with the intent of ensuring that my mother would not get the job. My performance failed and my mother got hired as a nurse's assistant at Grady Memorial Hospital where she worked with premature babies for 20 years.

When my mother took this job, everything changed. I became a latchkey kid. She worked the 3pm -11pm shift for her entire career which meant I had to walk to and from school and take on the full responsibility of being a student. Yes, I had siblings, but I was the last of eight and there's seven and a half years between me and my next oldest sibling. This means that support-time for my education was sliced and shared. My oldest sisters and brothers were either in high school, working jobs or becoming parents, and my nieces and nephews lived with us and were raised almost as my younger siblings. Time that probably should have been focused on my education was often devoted to them. What this meant was that I did what it took to pass from grade to grade. I was smart enough to survive, but I never thrived, and I was never challenged. Until sixth grade.

Enter Mrs. Sewell, a middle-aged White lady with platinum blond hair (although it looked grey to us). She would vehemently defend that it was indeed platinum blond! Here was this White lady teaching in a 99.9% Black school. She had scoliosis, which we all learned was curvature of the spine, and so did her daughter who was a flight attendant, a point of particular pride for her.

She held up the book *101 Poems* and said that we all had to buy a copy. I was in public school, and this was the first time that I had to find money to buy a book. I had enough of a challenge getting paper and pencils. She also told us we would be learning, from memory, over 60 poems, and that we had to learn them to pass. Gulp! She required that we purchase a specific type of composition book (another first) and at the end of each day, we would write a "new term" evaluation.

Abou Ben Adhem by Leigh Hunt was my entry into the remarkable world of poetry. To this day, anyone who was in Mrs. Sewell's class can recite most, if not all of that poem, even if we cannot remember any of the other poems, she made us learn.

Sylvia Sewell had such a profound impact on me. Her lessons took me from performing to transforming. I wasn't familiar with any of the poems I had to memorize but when it was time to stand and deliver, I would rise from my seat, proud and strong, and recite poetry in front of the class.

There were also the essays that introduced me to the world of free writing and storytelling, something I still do because it is so liberating. As I am writing this to you, I see how it was all connected, from me standing up and sharing the Sunday School lessons to reciting poems verbatim and learning to express myself in writing.

One day I had to stay after school for talking in class and the punishment was to write 100 times, "I will not talk in class" or something like that. ☺ I did not have paper and none of the other salty captives would lend me any. Mrs. Sewell had left the room, so without a way to complete the assignment, I left. Later that day I was playing baseball in my friend's backyard when someone ran to me and said "Dwight, Mrs. Sewell is at your house!" My heart dropped right out of my backside as my suppressed memories of being in trouble at school had made it into my play time. Yes, I got my butt whipped, and it hurt, but the point is what white female teacher in the 1970s would care so much about me as a student, that hours after work she would look up my address and come to my home to say that your education was much more important than a daily ritual. I did not necessarily appreciate it at the time, but I bet you, I never embarrassed my mother and sisters in that class again. Thank you, Mrs. Sewell, for caring this much for me. You changed my life!

And now, for my favorite pivotal moment. Here's the one that allowed me to, for the first time in my life, share my voice on the big stage.

Let's call it my *Benny and the Jets* moment

Pivotal Moment #3: Benny and the Jets (*Dedicated to the late Benny Hood*)

Today, whenever I meet with my classmates from the Benjamin E. Mays class of 1983 for our reunion or for drinks, someone is bound to bellow out in a high-pitched voice, "Benny, Benny, Benny and the Jets," and then those who were there for that defining moment will laugh and reminisce.

It was nearing the close of my sixth-grade school year at West Manor elementary. There was an opportunity to participate in an event that had never happened before or after in my grade school tenure. A talent show! A chance to stand in front of the entire school and strut your stuff.

I was fortunate that my older brothers were always buying great music (in the form of vinyl albums) from all types of artists; pop, rock, gospel, soul, local talent, you name it, it was in their collection. Michael Jackson, Peter Frampton, Earth, Wind and Fire and my favorite, Elton John. I would escape into these albums for hours and learn every word. This talent show gave me the chance to offer my karaoke skills to the world. There was no second guessing. Yes, I was going to do this! The artist was easy. Elton John! He was cool and talented, and his music touched my soul. Plus, I learned somewhere that his real name was Dwight.

The song was a difficult choice. *Your Song* was my favorite because of the passion and emotion behind the lyrics, but Benny and the Jets moved the crowd. Man, where were camera phones? The moment was epic! It was hot in the auditorium, and I was one of the last to perform. The talent that went up before me was not that great, and the audience was not impressed, especially the seventh graders, who could make this memory my worse one.

Here I was, the fat kid, dressed in a sand-colored, 3-piece suit and earth shoes. I handed my brother's album to a teacher praying it would not get scratched or that the needle wouldn't get stuck.

Lord, please help her find the right track and let the audience be able to hear the music coming from this single-speaker record player; and Lord, dear Lord, please don't let whoever's holding the microphone up to the speaker drop it thus causing the entire audience to erupt in embarrassing laughter that I will remember four decades later when I'm writing my big, famous book. Amen.

I was perspiring profusely. As I walked up the steps to the stage, I could already hear the laughter, but I traded my thick glasses for a pair of brown-tinted shades and transformed into Sir Elton John. Once the teacher finally got the track right and the music started, I was lost in the moment. I was above the crowd (that I couldn't see anyway) belting out the same passion and fire that I would have given if I were singing by myself. My voice had not changed, so yes, Elton and I could keep pace on even his highest notes. The crowd went wild, and history was made.

The next day, I was back to being tucked in the shell of my insecurities, but I had deposited something into the universe and into my schoolmates. I had bared my authentic self, which I believe is one of the keys to reaching your destiny. I knew the moment was high impact, but still, imagine my surprise when I found out that one of my classmates, a writer, and a poet, had captured it all in a poem:

Dwight Jones

is 😇 feeling blessed.

May 2, 2019 ·

Hey ya'll. I am feeling 10ft tall right now. Gayle Danley shared with me a poem that she wrote years ago about my West Manor 6th grade performance of Benny and the Jets. For those who were there, I am sure this will take you back. I also welcome my other classmates who may have heard the story, but since there were no camera phones back then, you could not enjoy the moment. I hope this brings the same smile to your face as it has done to mine. Thanks so much Gayle. This has blessed my heart!

"Here's the poem I wrote many, many years ago about that epic moment on West Manor's stage. Enjoy, as much as I enjoyed that memorable moment."

The Light
There wasn't much light on stage that day
But when the curtains parted a half inch
and a brown boy stepped before the audience
it was as if a spotlight flooded his face
Hey kids shake it loose together
The spotlight's hittin' something that's been known to change the weather
Dwight Jones
cornbread brown
glasses reflecting what little light there was
silver tooth smile
We had never heard him sing
so even the air held its breath
I swear I could hear his heartbeat
that morning at the talent show:
She's got electric boots
a mohair suit
Notes bold and shy
rose from his throat like mist off the river

His body rocking to its own rhythm
what was this song and who had this 12 year old boy become inside of it?
But they're so spaced out
He sang to himself
he sang to us
And we heard him
We caught the beauty of him within our eyes
His song was not perfect:
Some of us snickered beneath the Snickers snuck beneath our teeth
some dreaded the butt whooping that awaited the arrival home
But the piano was on fire
The drumbeat shimmered against our skin
Darkness disappeared
in that one kaleidoscopic moment:
Bennie
Bennie
Bennie
Bennie Bennie Bennie and the
Jets
Light washed over him
like a baptism of sound and passion
and he was saved
no longer just a boy
but a promise uttered in the chamber of those who had come before and those who would come after him
We were saved that day
each of us
songs
melodies
hymns
now
worth
singing.

Pivotal Moment #4: Highschool 8th – 12th grade

Overall, I consider my high school experience a great one. I wasn't a super student. I didn't have a wonderful plan, but I had a strong family, and I lived in a community where people cared about me. Most of my teachers were wonderful people, and my classmates and our school culture were more than admirable. I lived in a thriving city full of Black leaders who were making history and changing the world, so much so, that I did not realize Black people were really a minority until I went to college. In elementary and high school, I did not have to face systematic oppression. However, it was there waiting for me, day one, at college.

I attended Southwest High school from eighth to tenth grade then Mays High from 11th to 12th. Back then, there weren't any middle schools in Atlanta. You were in elementary from K – 7th, then you went to high school from 8th – 12th grade. I can't remember if high school had just started, but on August 30th, 1978, my father passed away from lung cancer. My foundation was taken from me. The strength of my family, what it meant to be a Jones, my daddy, my hero was gone. This was a pivotal time for me. I had every opportunity and excuse to take a destructive path, but my Heavenly Father saved me, ensuring that I felt His presence and knew that He was there. I looked to him to fill the role of my father.

I can remember, maybe a year after my father died, having an episode of uncontrollable tears and grief in my bedroom. I was overcome by this hollow feeling of being abjectly alone. But that day, a year after losing my father, while in my room, I was overtaken by the sense of a blanket being laid on me and I felt comforted. I knew that I was not alone. I believe it was the Holy Spirit soothing me. I knew that help was there, and that God saw me, if no one else did. Did my circumstance change? No. Did I continue to have more failures than successes? Yes. But I had hope and that was enough.

I am reminded of this scripture which I hope brings you as much comfort as it did me:

Matthew 11:28 – 30: *"Come to Me, all you who labor and are heavy laden, and I will give you rest. Take My yoke upon you and learn from Me, for I am gentle and lowly in heart, and you will find rest for your souls. For My yoke is easy and My burden is light."*

Back to high school: I was fatherless. My mother worked the night shift my entire childhood, so I was not anyone's priority. I did my best to maintain a facade of an existence. I was okay at a lot of things, but not great at anything...except Army ROTC where I made all A's because it made sense to me. It provided the structure and discipline I needed. I was rewarded for my hard work: best drilled platoon; raising the most money for charity; best drilled company. Still the narrative for my future was bleak.

By my 11th grade year, I knew I wanted to go to college, but I had no one to guide me there. Not my football coaches, not my family. No one. I went to the school guidance counsellor for help and direction.

I apparently had unknowingly offended my PhD guidance counsellor at some point. I would joke with her a lot, with my 16-year-old playfulness, and call her Johnny Cash. She never corrected me. She always smiled when I teasingly called her out of her name. I remember our meeting so vividly. I'd made an appointment with her to talk about college. I was lost, I needed help and I completely trusted her counsel and support.

Well, things didn't pan out the way I'd envisioned: she had my file on her desk, to her left. She peered at it for only a few seconds, and with a bit of a smile she said, "Dwight, you will probably be dead or in jail by 21."

I don't remember any other words from that meeting, just politely leaving. I felt like the remaining light on a cigarette butt crushed under the heel of her black pump. I was broken and I was alone.

I thought my narrative had been written and the book had been closed.

I finished high school as a decent football player, Cadet Captain, and company commander in the Army ROTC. I was smart enough to get by in my classes, but I did not have enough support or encouragement to push me from good student to great student. I had two colleges that were interested in offering me scholarships. Fort Valley State, that brought me in on a college recruiting trip and told me that they wanted me to play there, and Marion Military Institution in Marion, Alabama where I could pursue my military aspirations. When I told my high school coaches that Fort Valley wanted me to play, I did not know what to expect. I guess I was hoping that one of them would sit me down and say "that's great! Now you need to do steps 1,2 and 3." I guess these are the things your father would normally help you with. Needless to say, I did not receive any help or instruction, so that dream died on the vine. At least I still had ROTC.

I went to my commanding officer, Ret. LT Colonel Newton. I took all of my brochures and letters and told him about my scholarship offers. I thought he would be proud. I scored really high on the Armed Services Vocational Aptitude Battery (ASVAB) military assessment test. I had a decent SAT score, and I was good in ROTC. Now Colonel Newton was White and spoke with a southern accent. I never saw him as racist. I saw him as a leader, a male in a position of authority.

He took the brochure and turned to the page of the graduating class. He said, "son look at this picture and tell me what you don't see". The picture was shot from the back, and all I could see were shaved white heads. I searched for the contrast of a black pate, but I don't remember spotting any. Maybe one or two. He asked: "what do you think your chances are of graduating from a place like this in southern Alabama?" I got the point. And even though that college continued to pursue me, his words, and movies like

TAPS, where I saw how Black students were treated, had me terrified of that place.

Now I don't know if Colonel Newton's counsel was good or bad. I only know that I did not have the courage or support system to take on the challenge on my own. Have you ever been told *no* for an aspiration or goal by someone you trust and admire? How would you stay positive and keep moving forward when the people in your support system don't believe in you? Where do you turn when the road is full of dead ends and detours?

Pivotal Moment #5: College Years – Georgia State University (GSU)

My college years are more of a blur, but when I was playing Spades or eating burgers from the B&D (Bite & Die) cafeteria, I know that I was really engaged! Georgia State University was my first exposure to an America where Black people were a minority. It was 14% Black, and the average age of students was higher than 26. There I was, the seventeen-year-old, proud product of an all-Black community with an educational experience that was 99.9% Black. Unfortunately, GSU made sure, from day one, that I was a number and that there was no real concern about whether I graduated or not.

I did not do any college preparatory work to try to find the right school for me. I simply went to Georgia State because my grades were good enough and my brother Taft had gone there before me. After the Air Force, he was able to earn his bachelor's in Business Administration. Without support, I felt like my options were limited, so when I took the SAT, I made sure they got my scores, I applied in my senior year of high school, and they accepted me. Had I known the average age of students was twenty-six at the time, I'm sure that I would have tried another route.

I'd received my acceptance letter prior to high school graduation, so I knew which school I'd be going to. I had the GPA and the SAT scores to make my acceptance very smooth. However, after the acceptance letter, there was absolutely no additional communications. None, until a week before classes when I went to the registrar's office. They found me in the system and offered no explanation for their failure to communicate with me. I was told that I had to take a basic entrance exam THAT DAY to be placed in my classes. I believe this was unfair and racist. *I had to take an exam cold* after three months of partying and trying to forget high school. Had I known this, of course I would have studied. As expected, without preparation, I did poorly, which relegated me to two years of remedial, non-credit courses that pretty much ensured that I would not graduate. This setback made it take two years for me to get to my first freshman course!

Many of my high school classmates who attended HBCU's (Historically Black Colleges and Universities) or PWI's (Predominately White Institutions), were able to transfer to GSU well ahead of me because I was still in remedial classes. Even though my high school performance and SAT scores might have been higher than theirs. I felt trapped; a poor Black man trying to pay his own way through school but headed for failure. Despite this misfortune, I soldiered on as best I could.

To graduate from Georgia State, every student must pass the state regents exam. It can be a daunting task for some. Many do not pass it after multiple attempts and there are support classes for those cases. I felt like the fact that I passed the regence exam on my first attempt (while still being tied to remedial classes) is evidence that I did not belong in the remedial courses in the first place. Knowing this didn't change my circumstances, but at least I knew I was better than the box that GSU had placed me in.

I made tons of friends on campus, deflecting my pain through social acceptance. Most of us were in the same boat. We'd meet up daily in the Sparks Hall student center across from the bookstore.

One pivotal move I made when I was 18 was pledging my fraternity, Kappa Alpha Psi. This brotherhood placed me in the company of young Black men who were striving to be "excellent in every field of human endeavor" and helped me mature into a man. I learned how to study, the importance of timeliness and that there was no place for excuses. Our line name was "Six Masters of Perseverance" because we had to withstand more than your average obstacles to join the fraternity. I think this was also a fundamental lesson for my life ahead. But by far, the *most* pivotal moment from my college years happened two years after I got out of developmental studies.

That's when I found a program called Business Information Processing that introduced me to technology and started me on my technical journey. I landed my first job in technology while taking my Orientation to Computers course. I also took programming courses in Basic, Cobol, and Report Program Generator (RPGIII), then Statistics and computer operations courses. In the beginning, I was nearing academic probation, but in the end, I only made A's and B's.

After four years of college and only two years of progress, I made the gut-wrenching decision to drop out. I chose to marry my sweetheart. A year later my first child Jarah was born. Something had to give. Four years of paying my way through college, working full time and marriage on top of all that. I chose family love and devotion over my formal education.

But I had found my calling.

Pivotal Moment #6: My Professional Journey

On what would have been my father's 63rd birthday, March 3rd, 1986, I began my journey as a technologist. My first role was as a third shift assistant computer operator for Financial Services Corporation. I was in my third year at Georgia State University, a very lost Business Administration major, losing the battle of paying my own tuition while working full-time. To say I was struggling academically would be putting it mildly! Up until this point I had never made above a C. But I found a program (Business Information Processing) and something about computers awoke the sleeper in me.

In my first course, Orientation to Computers, I earned my first A at Georgia State, and I never made less than a B in the program. One of my assignments was to interview the head of an IT department. My sister was a data processor and arranged a meeting for me and Mr. Brad Thomas, the Director of Management Information Systems at Financial Services Corporation. In my heart of hearts, I dreamed that this would provide an open door for me.

Being a Kappa, I knew how to dress to impress! I was fly in my blue suit, crisply-starched white button-down collar shirt and gold tie. I had my list of questions for Mr. Thomas but about halfway through, he mentioned that he had a role opening up and asked if I would be interested. With all the courage inside me, I told him I would love to discuss it after we completed my list of questions. After my interview with my first manager Brent Guyton, I got the job! The struggling student landed his first professional job, and the start date was on my late father's birthday, March 3rd. This was the opportunity I had been praying for. I did not take it for granted.

In six months, I was promoted to computer operator. I was promoted four times in five years. Because I ran the nightly batch processing, I documented all of the interactions between the different technologies. In those days, all of your tech was housed in computer rooms, with raised floors and expensive cooling systems.

Your mainframe or minicomputer Central Processing Units (CPUs) were housed separately from your disk drives, your tape drives, and your printers. I managed an IBM 4361, a Wang VS 2200, Burroughs, and Unisys XE520s. There were no direct connections between computing platforms; they were all unique and proprietary. We used reel-to-reel tape drives for input and output between systems. Some computers understood ASCII and others EBCDIC, so if I wanted my Unisys platform to talk to IBM, I had to convert input from ASCII to a separate output tape to EBCDIC so the IBM tape drives could read them. To produce reports, we had to batch-process jobs. There was nightly processing that fed into weekly, monthly, quarterly, and annual processing jobs.

We printed reports on huge cases of green bar paper. To get three copies, you printed on three-part paper with carbon in the middle. Once your print job finished, you used a decollator to separate and remove the carbon for copy one. Then you had to repeat the process for copies two and three. After that, the green bar paper was connected by perforation, and you needed to take each copy through a bursting machine to produce separate pages. This form of processing was methodical, and you could not make missteps. Back up and restores were imperative as system crashes happened often. There was no such thing as redundancy and high availability. If you had a system crash, you had to depend on tape backups to bring your system as close to current as possible, then you had to run batch program jobs again for any missing days. I became so intimate with the processing of these systems that when our company was acquired, they leveraged my documentation and I was promoted to Operations Analyst, where I was selected as one of eight to continue with the company after layoffs that took the jobs of 40 of my co-workers. Soon after, the work of those four systems was replaced by a single Unix box running Informix SQL. This 4th generation language, processed in real-time, all of the work of the batch processing systems. I also learned technical support and how to build the cabling for cluster communications for the XE520s, coax for the IBM terminals, and I even built my first IBM token ring PC based network!

My next opportunity in technology was at Decatur Federal Savings and Loans where I was a Technical Resource Specialist II. I learned so much about data communications in this role, implementing and supporting banking systems and data-line connectivity over switched 56k networks. In those days, before the invention of wireless networking, not only did you run the cable drops, but you also built the cables and patched and supported the installations. I was dispatched support for bank teller line and platform systems, ATMs, back-office Local Area Networks (LANs) and terminal systems. At Decatur Federal, I became a LAN expert owning all Novell Netware Networks. I received numerous awards and commendations for outstanding customer service and was promoted once. I left Decatur Federal because they were going through a similar downsizing effort that I'd experienced at FSC, and it was too emotional seeing my friends and colleagues losing their jobs.

I interviewed for a Network and Telecommunications Manager job for WH Smith and won the role. WH Smith is a more than 200-year-old company out of the United Kingdom that started their US headquarters in Atlanta, Ga. This was my first opportunity to build out an enterprise system from end to end. I took what started as eight PCs and designed, deployed, and supported them until they became a 250 PC Local Area Network connecting to 400 retail locations. I was responsible for the AT&T G3i Telephone communication system and all store communications. In addition, I managed the interoperations of systems including Novell LANs, Data General, SCO Unix, and HP 9000 mid ranges, supporting Informix SQL, Point of Sales, Inventory management and financial systems.

From 1997 to 2002, I transitioned into becoming a consultant. During this period, I made a significant leap in technical expertise and take-home pay. I learned that the more certs (certifications) you obtain, the more money you could command. My first consulting role was for Bank of America, where I was a Senior Systems Architect. I developed, tested, and implemented the first Windows Server Domain Architecture for their National Direct Call Center, replacing their Novell Netware environment. I was responsible for design-prototyping, development and quality assurance testing, rack buildout and installation of the Compaq 42u servers and roles. I wrote all initial build documentation, technical notes, standards, and procedures. During this time, I started studying the Microsoft Certified Professional program and followed the path to become a Microsoft Certified Systems Engineer.

My next consulting role was for Norfolk Southern Railway where I was a Senior Network Engineer, providing support for the LAN/WAN platform and the enterprise customer base as well as support for transportation systems in an open environment consisting of Windows Server, Novell, Unix, and IBM hosts systems. This is where I was first introduced to Cisco routers and switches and began to pivot my learning toward Cisco Certifications. I became a Cisco Certified Design Associate, Network Associate, Design Professional, Network Professional. I also passed the written certification test to become a Cisco Certified Internetworking Expert. I supported Norfolk Southern systems through the huge challenge of Y2k.

My final consulting job before joining Microsoft was with Bell South Internet Services. I was a Senior Network Engineer for the Network Deployment / Infrastructure provisioning team. I was the only consultant lead on the Infrastructure Provisioning Core team. I was awarded for outstanding job performance, and I also received a certificate of excellence. I led, without incident, the forklift migrations for their entire business management facility supporting their growth as an Internet Service Provider.

So why am I telling you all this? It's not to brag; it's to let you see all the steps I had to take to land where I am now. I was definitely not an overnight success. You can look at my climb like it's a trudge through the vines of my career. One thick vine led to the next and even though I was afraid at times, I kept on climbing.

Chapter 4: NEVER GIVE UP!

Over the next several chapters, I want to pour into you the hard-won knowledge that made my tech journey different from others in the field. You see, I knew a lot of people who began their technology trek in the same place that I did. We all heard the buzz about technology being a great career path and that there were more jobs than people to fill them. We were told you can start right out of college and make a six-figure salary. All that is very true. However, I know too many Black people who graduated with technology degrees, many with honors and others with straight A's. They were brilliant by any measure, and many of them are successful to this day; however, they all had to find paths outside of technology. Some turned to business or real-estate, and others landed jobs in law enforcement.

Why and how did the door for many Blacks close for technical careers? Seriously, no one goes to college to earn a bachelor's or master's in computer science to work for the sheriff's department. If I spend time and money on an education to become a doctor, guess what I want to do when I earn my degree? Be a darn doctor! Unfortunately, and systemically, many brilliant Black people have not been able to survive the early challenges and reap the ripe fruit that high tech provides.

While colleges are busy graduating the next class of Black technologists, I am losing count of the grads, and industry hires, who only last a couple of years and then they're gone.

How am I different and why did I manage to stay in a field that dashes the dreams of so many? After all, I did not finish college and I was not born into wealth and privilege.

I say again: I stand on the shoulders of giants. Watching my father fight for the right to expand his business was a gift that I can only *try* to share with you in words. I am sure his victory placed him among other *firsts* for African Americans. My dad should have been able to go to the state capital like any other man and apply for this license, but because he was Black, he was told no over and over again. I still have the articles from the *Wall Street Journal* and the *New York Times* that document how he lost his seventh appeal, but he did not quit. Even if it meant taking his request to the President of the United States, which he did, and Lordhavemercy! he got his I.C.C. license.

He never lost confidence in himself or his ability. He never lost sight of his dream. He was passionate about two things: this country and driving trucks. He was proud of his service in the Army and his participation in the European theatre. He leveraged what he learned as a military driver, supplying our troops in a different country, to being beloved and respected in his community for his truck driving skills. He believed in his gift and would not let his light be extinguished. Even on his deathbed, he was trying to reestablish his business. He shared with my oldest brother the things that needed to be done to keep his dream alive.

Right here, I want to deposit one scripture and three takeaways. The scripture is Romans 8:31 (paraphrased and made personal), if God be for you, who can be against you? And here are three nuggets I want you to tuck inside your heart.

> 1. Never give up
> 2. Learn perseverance
> 3. Pace yourself

These have been key to my journey, helping me push past the no's and bringing me back to the fight in those times when I found myself on the losing side of layoffs and economic downturns.

There are a couple of quotes from noted authors that I carry with me: Edwin Louis Cole wrote in *Maximized Manhood*, "champions aren't those that never fail, but those that never quit!".

Paraphrasing Elbert Willis, the minister and author who said that "your belief must be like a cork. You can take a cork down under hundreds of feet of water and just hold it there, but what happens when you move your hand? It is going to pop right back to the surface."

Let me tell you about my first chance to quit. My first tech job came to a very emotional end. This was the company where, in five years, I was promoted four times and by the time I was 24, I co-lead operations. The company had been purchased by Mutual of New York and had changed the entire batch processing multi system platform to a single UNIX mid-range, running Informix SQL. This was a 4th generation computing platform that did real-time processing which took an entire Management Information Systems department to support. The day we found out about the acquisition, approximately thirty people lost their jobs. There were a lot of tears and heartbreak. At that time, downsizing was a new thing. People were still in the mindset that you could work for a single company until retirement, and, up to that point, Financial Services Corporation was that type of company. However, they were impacted by the 1987 stock market decline and did not recover.

There were approximately twenty people in my department who did not lose their jobs, and initially, I was one of eight that would be the new IT department. The remaining twelve were given layoff-incentivized packages to keep working but with a future layoff date. Unfortunately, a few months later, I found out that the VP of IT, his admin, and I were also going to be laid off. I was working my way out of my great job. When my job ended, I went from being the person that worked hard, co-leading computer operations, back to the ground floor of failure.

I am a college dropout, and one of two Blacks in the technology department. At that point, I had a family, so it was time to get a job in line with who I really was. So, I started washing cars because I felt like I was an imposter in the corporate world. I knew that I could labor so I began to detail cars for members of my church.

One day my pastor's wife, the late Sister Geraldine Thompson, asked me to wash her car, which I was honored to do. Word was getting out about my car washing business, and how I would put my all into every car. There was one problem. Sister Gerri's car did not have the best paint job and when I put the high-pressure hose on it, the pinstriping started blowing off. OMG! I tried to hand wax it and the wax would not come off. What is this?? I was living hand to mouth, and I knew I could not afford to fix the car. I was not bonded or insured. Most of all, I was so embarrassed and ashamed for messing up the car of someone I really cared for.

I explained to Sister Gerri what happened and waited to talk to her husband, Pastor Wayne C. Thompson. What was he going to say? I knew he was mad. I saw him come out of her office and I walked to meet him as a man. "Pastor Wayne, I don't know what happened. I am so sorry for destroying the paint on your wife's car." He simply said, "I forgive you."

I did not know how to process that. I had ruined his wife's paint job. I was already at the bottom and deserved to be jumped on. After all, my high school counselor, my commanding officer, and my college administrators had all affirmed that losing was my place.

The pastor took a moment (when he should have pounced) and instead chose to lift me up. It felt as if he was laying down his life for mine in that moment.

A couple of days later, he called me and asked me out to lunch. I met him at the church and we drove off in his Mercedes S500 (that I did not want to even touch, let alone ride in). Over lunch he asked, "what happened to your technical job?" I explained that I had been laid off and was not able to find anything. I shared that I did not have a college degree and that because of how tough the market was, I could not compete for technical jobs. He then asked who helped me get the first job without a college degree? And I said, "God did." The next thing he said opened my eyes and rerouted my compass from South to North. "If God gave you the last job, why do you not believe that He can give you the next one?" That was all I needed to hear. I immediately went back to getting the Sunday paper, looking for technical jobs and mailing resumes, something this generation knows nothing about. One of the jobs I applied for was at Decatur Federal Savings & Loans.

You know, one of the things that I have learned about being a child of God is that when He has something for you, He has a way of showing you that it was Him alone. After printing and mailing a batch of resumes, I noticed that the printer had cut off half of my resume. You guessed it...the one that went to Decatur Federal was in the bad batch, but I did not notice this error until after it was mailed.

So, first miracle – on a Friday, I got a call from Decatur Federal based on a half-printed resume. Now Decatur Federal is a bank, so no one works on the weekend.

Miracle number two - I was sitting down with my wife and children eating one of those amazing Sunday dinners, and the phone was ringing. I was going to let it go to voicemail, but my wife spoke to me in a tone that didn't even sound like her voice. It sounded more like she was one of the Bene Gesserits, you know those priest ladies from the movie *Dune* when they use "the voice" and it commands you to do something that you had no intention of doing.

"Pick up the phone!" I started walking to the phone, looking back at her. When I answered, it was HR from Decatur Federal asking me to come in for an interview the next day. I interviewed and got the job the same day! To God be the Glory!

Miracle number three - as a tech support specialist, one of my first incidents was in the HR department. I cannot remember the name of the lady that hired me, but after I fixed her computer and was about to walk out of the office, I passed a stack of what looked like more than 200 resumes. I noticed them because the stack was so high. Without prompting, the HR manager asked, "do you know what that stack of papers are?" I said no. She said, "those are all the people that applied for your role." I shared with her how grateful I was for the opportunity, all the while thinking *if God be for you, who can be against you?*

What am I trying to say? There will be setbacks, obstacles, economic downturns, poor managers, bad fits, layoffs, and firings. I have been through them all, and you'll experience your share of them, but keep your eyes on Jesus. He will get you through. Life is a marathon, not a sprint. If you receive a *no*, it just may be no *for now*, or perhaps whatever you are going for is not God's best for you. You must outlast the no's. I have developed the skill of perseverance; therefore, bad breaks cannot defeat me.

There was another economic downturn for technologists right before I joined Microsoft. I had reached a technical plateau. I was six figures. I was billing $85 an hour at Bell South Internet Services and was the only consultant on their core engineering team. I was a Microsoft Certified Systems Engineer, and I had passed the Cisco Certified Internetworking Expert written exam. I was smart, appreciated and part of a great team. Then the Dot Bomb era hit and because of improper accounting practices, companies were no longer able to carry consultants as part of their CAPEX, capitalized expenses that made a company show that they were invested in growth. Here I was, pulling $170k per year before overtime, and BellSouth told me that they had to end my contract and offered me a job for $65k! That was an insult to me, and I politely thanked them and walked away. But you know it is so true," pride comes before the fall." Because of the downturn, I could not find work anywhere...and I mean anywhere. I couldn't even land a job parking cars for AVIS!

I was so distressed that one day, after dropping my daughter off at school and taking my car to a repair shop, I just decided to walk home. Thirteen miles. My best friend and fraternity brother called me. "Man, what is wrong with you? What are you doing?"

"I just need to walk man. I can't find work. I have six children to feed."

Thank goodness, Robert brought me in to work in his daycare centers. This was lifesaving and allowed me to cover my mortgage and keep food on the table.

I actually loved every moment of working with him, his wife, and those kids. I served unto the Lord while some of his other employees were angry and disgruntled. I told them how privileged I was to work there every day. He had my back, and I had his. It was a precious time to connect with my friends and their parents who also worked in the business. Every time his wife Kenya would see me, she would say, "God has something great waiting for you!" I had heard it before; I knew it was true. I was going through the fire, but this time I had a fire hydrant called hope. Now, to be totally honest, I was mad that I had to go through it, but I had seen what God could do for me. I knew that I belonged to Him.

About two years after losing my contract, countless resumes sent and near misses, I began desperately sending resumes outside of the Atlanta area. I was looking for work anywhere. I had interviewed for the American Cancer Society, and they wanted to hire me, but they had problems funding the role. It took about a year of calling the hiring manager every two weeks to check, but I landed the job for, you guessed it, $65k a year, the exact same amount I walked away from at BellSouth! I gladly took the role and wasn't two weeks in when a Microsoft recruiter (Tim Talley) called me and asked if I wanted to come to Redmond to interview for a role! They made me an offer I could not refuse. Six figures, relocation package, stock, and bonus. Plus, initial housing and a couple of roundtrips back and forth for me, my wife and my six children.

When God does it, there are no questions.

Eighteen years later and I am still here. I started as a Network Engineer for MSN Global Network Services. Then I relocated back to Atlanta as a Senior Engagement Manager for the BellSouth and AT&T account bringing AT&T U-verse to market before joining the team I am on today in Microsoft Digital (formerly Microsoft IT). I was recently promoted to principal program manager.

The challenge today is that most people have a microwave mentality. If the meal is not ready in three minutes or if *Door Dash* is late, they are upset. Well, when I was growing up, the most delicious Sunday meals were prepared right after the prior Sunday's meal. Cooking may have started as early as Friday! The house would be full of the aroma and anticipation of the collard greens, yams, black-eyed peas, corn bread, deviled eggs, and fried chicken just a few agonizing minutes from our plates. You can't microwave any of that goodness nor the gratitude and appreciation for that soulful labor of love.

I shared my journey in the article below. I hope that it inspires you and encourages you on your exciting road ahead. Remember "if God be for you, who can be against you?" Never give up! Practice the art of perseverance, and please pace yourself. All good things take time.

NEVER GIVE UP!

MY MICROSOFT STORY OF PERSEVERANCE

FROM LEVEL 60 TO PRINCIPAL -- 17 YEARS IN THE MAKING!

On November 19, 2020, at exactly 2:28 PM PST with 2 minutes remaining in my connect meeting, my manager shared his screen and showed me that I was being promoted to principal. I was so overcome with emotion; I could not speak. Tears flowed and would not stop. All I could do was show my appreciation and end the call after which I continued to shed tears for the remainder of the day. I am still emotional about the moment and tears are forming as I type even now. You see I had resolved in my heart that I would not reach the principal level as a Microsoft employee. I started as an entry level engineer, I turned 55 on November 3rd, and I am an African American man. So, I thought that senior would be my career plateau. Even though I was being mentored, coached, and sponsored, I had very low trust in any of it because of many, many years of attempts and closed doors.

I'd endured so many broken promises and took my share of paths that almost ended my employment with other teams. Before I came to Microsoft Digital, which was then Microsoft IT, I worked for a group that no longer exists called Microsoft TV. I took the level 64 Sr. Engagement Manager role when I was still level 61, fresh off a paygrade promotion from my beloved MSN Networking team. I took this job because it allowed me to relocate my family back to Atlanta from Redmond. I was also promised that I would be allowed to prove my value and rapidly up-level to the 64-pay grade. I surely did all the level 64 work!

Although I over delivered in that role for nearly three years, my manager would not fight for me. I was never up- leveled. I took a $50k account for Microsoft to a $460M account that brought 48% profit margins, but my manager only gave me average reviews. What made things worse was when my customer moved operations to Texas, I was told I had 30 days to find another job in Microsoft or I would be terminated. I was hurt, angry and afraid, however, I reached out and got offers from both my former MSN team and Microsoft IT. I chose Microsoft IT and took the position of level 61 Service Manager. My family remained in GA, and I rented an apartment near Redmond. It took more than 2 years to sort out the logistics to get my family back to Redmond with me and, as you can imagine I was bitter and angry that I had worked a level 64 role as a 61, nearly lost my family in the process and I had to take a role at the same level as when I left.

Well, I had to change my mindset. Instead of being bitter, I changed my thinking to become better. Through lots of lessons, I made the most of working in Microsoft IT and used all the experience I gained to my benefit. I began challenging myself and my managers to give me the most difficult, complex projects and services because I wanted to prove my worth. This won me the CIO award in 2013 under my managers Toby Smith & Tom Foster. I even moved 3 levels from 2008 – 2015!

Then there was the elusive principal level. God only knows how many interviews and "near misses" I had trying to reach that that heavenly level. How many new hires and promotions I watched, thinking why not me? As I look back, there were four key things that opened the door for me.

First, I landed on a team that I loved and believed in, EE (Employee Experience under Nathalie D'Hers), doing what I loved to do as a Service Engineer. Second, I had a manager that believed in me and who always told me the truth. Yes, my work was strong enough for the principal level, I was told, but realistically there would not be any principal roles in my current discipline. Third, I found a sponsor and a mentor who both really cared about me and nurtured me through all the distrust of not seeing many people like me raised to that level. Finally, I invested in external coaching which helped me ask my managers and myself tough and uncomfortable questions. It also helped me make the hard career shift that forced me to trust a process that had hurt me in the past.

Two and a half years later, it all paid off.

Here is my **actual email** to Nathalie, Dan, Sean and Senthil:

"I am almost done crying! ☺ *Seriously I cannot put into words how grateful I am for this moment. This level was an impossible dream to me, and I had really reconciled in my heart that I would not make it to the principal level. Dan, Sean, I cannot put into words how thankful I am for the faith and the hours of investment, mentorship, sponsorship and coaching that you all have put into me. Nathalie, I love your heart and the vision and culture of our team. I feel at home and with family on this team.*

I humbly thank you all so very much, because as it relates to this promotion, there is no me without you!"

Dwight Jones and Family

Chapter 5:
SUPERSTARS AND HEROES: BLACK PEOPLE IN TECHNOLOGY!

This chapter is all about showing you how Black people all over the world have never stopped innovating and making technological advances before slavery and especially today. I want to broadcast, loud and proud, how many of these technical contributions are fundamental to the success of companies like RING, ADT, Amazon, Google, Microsoft, and countless others. The inventions of these outstanding pioneers improve the quality of our lives every day. Here are six of my favorite examples along with the love and respect I carry in my heart for these giants in innovation who paved a smooth path for us all to follow.

1. Granville T. Woods – Inventor of the Telegraph – 1887 (173) Columbus Neighborhoods: Inventor Granville T. Woods – YouTube

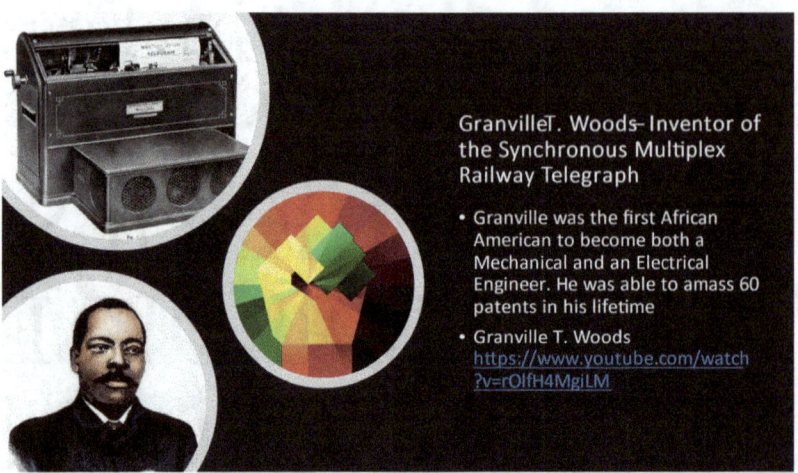

Granville T Woods is a forefather of electrical and mechanical engineers. He has over 60 patents to his name. Granville invented Synchronous Multiplex Railway Telegraph and the third rail used by subways today for communication. In the early days of railway transportation, there was no way for trains to communicate. As a result, railway incidents were common. Through Granville's telegraph system, messages could be sent to train engineers communicating track conditions and other messages. Think about how fundamental the telegraph system is to communication today. As America grew, messages could be sent from town to town. His invention was foundational for telephone communication.

Because of greed and racism, many of Granville's ideas were stolen by corporations that continue to make millions, while he had to spend his life fighting to prove that he was the inventor. If you know the brand GE and Westinghouse, you should also know the name Granville T Woods. In my technical journey, it was presented to me early on that "communication is the key". I believe that you can follow the communication thread to see technical advancement from generation to generation and its catalyst to improve the human condition.

You can start with voice and drums, but move to papyrus and hieroglyphic script, to one of Granville's society-changing inventions. Knowing that this Black man was able to advance such an amazing invention during slavery blows my mind. We should learn his story and communicate, communicate, communicate. **Not having the names of the next set of inventors as common as Elon Musk or Bill Gates, really lets me know that there is something terribly wrong with our society.**

There are terms that corporations throw around that really put the inventor at a disadvantage. "Think Differently" or "Build on Others" have, at the core, someone else's idea. You may have the money or resources to expand and benefit, but it was still someone's original idea that is not reflected in your making money from this idea. Let's break it down and make it plain. We should always be able to tie the invention to the original creator.

Let me get off of my soapbox! I want this message to be an enlightening one. I want you to see, in plain sight, the technology originators (the Real Old G's!) that corporations benefit from every day.

2. Jesse Eugene Russell – Inventor of the digital cell phone – 1988 https://www.youtube.com/watch?v=WmNHH-361dyA

That's right! The digital signaling that is allowing your smartphone to be smart was created by Mr. Russell. There were mobile phones before Mr. Russell, but they were using an analogue signal and tied to the car. Mr. Russell's invention is the reason you are able to carry your phone in your pocket. He created the digital cellular base station and the fiber optic microcell utilizing high power linear amplifier technology and digital modulation techniques, which enabled new digital services for cellular mobile users. Mr. Russell has over 100 patents to his name.

3. Dr. James West - Inventor of the Electret Microphone used in mobile phones and computers –1962 https://www.youtube.com/watch?v=95EFhuRyAe0

There were microphones before Dr. West's invention, but they were costly, large, and used a lot of power. In 1962, Dr. West invented the electret microphone, a miniature microphone that does not need a battery. Yes, like the one in your cell phone, computer, and in spy movies. As a matter of fact, Dr. West's design is used in 90% of contemporary microphones manufactured today.

4. Dr. Marian Croak – Inventor of Voice over IP (VOIP) technology used by Skype, Teams, Zoom and mobile devices - 1973 https://www.youtube.com/watch?v=4kUmEpBNWXQ

Dr. Croak invented Voice over Internet Protocol technology in 1973. This is the technology that allows us to use *Skype, Teams,* and Zoom over our PC and mobile devices to communicate over the Internet. Dr. Croak's invention is near and dear to my heart. I spent many years as a network engineer and have held professional and expert level certifications. I was an expert in TCP/IP networking and routing. I delivered the core networking design for BellSouth Internet Services. I also designed and deployed the MSN Messenger deployments for Microsoft. I was part of the team that brought Skype for Business and Microsoft Teams to life. Not once in my professional learnings or career did I hear Dr. Croak's name mentioned. This lady is a global treasure. Where would we be without her in this time of pandemic where we are able to use Teams, Zoom or our mobile devices to work from home? She deserves a Nobel peace prize. Learn her name and mention her on your next Zoom call.

5. Gerry Lawson – Invented the first cartridge-based gaming system – 1976 https://www.youtube.com/watch?v=n7ZE-X-EvBA

The gaming industry is a multi-billion-dollar industry. Brands like *Xbox*, *PlayStation,* and *Sega* have created loyal followings and have made it okay to be an adult and play games. It's amazing that in the mid-1980s one of my first jobs was in an arcade (named 2001) in the Galleria Mall in Atlanta. I started as a cook, but later became the first Black game floor host. This was a foreshadowing of things to come as I was responsible for the maintenance of those huge arcade games (i.e., *Pacman, Donkey Kong, Frogger, Galaga, Dig Dug* and the rest), keeping the token machines operational and providing general floor customer service.

Little did I know that Gerry Lawson was the inventor of many of these games. Nor did I know that he invented the first cartridge-based gaming system. Think about it: every cartridge or CD ROM-based game was originated by the great Mr. Lawson. What I am most proud of was that I did not have to stumble across Mr. Lawson's name because *Xbox* was having a convention where they shared his story. What an honor to work for a company that acknowledged this Black man's contribution to success! Thank you, Microsoft (*Xbox*), for doing this. Let's continue to tell his story.

6. Staying with our communication theme, the last Black inventor that I am going to highlight is Marie Van Brittan Brown – Invented the first CCTV Video Surveillance System –1966 https://www.youtube.com/watch?v=0-F798nGoOg

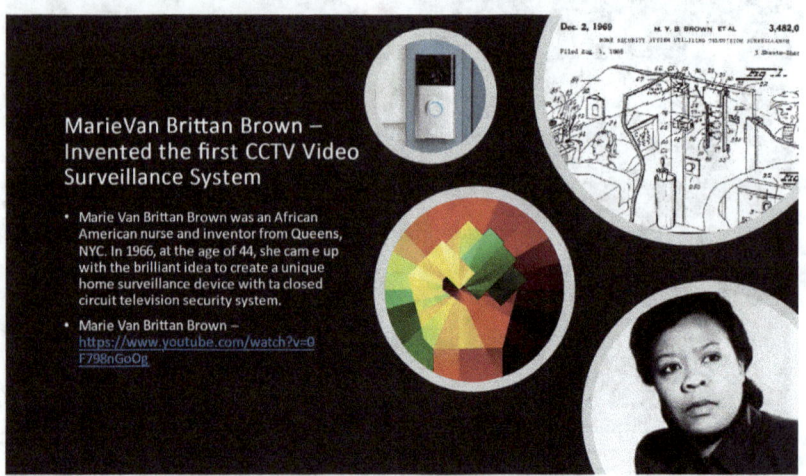

What I love most about Ms. Brown's story is that she was not a technologist. She was a nurse, but her ideas and patent were so technically complex that the model still holds today. Ms. Brown invented the first CCTV Video Surveillance System. Think about what RING, ADT or any security system does today. She invented that! From the camera system to the two-way communications with the camera system, to the ability to notify the police or fire department in the event of intrusion, she invented that. Marie should also have a Nobel Peace prize.

I have just shared with you six examples of inventions from brilliant African Americans that have taken communication to epic levels and redefined world culture. These examples prove that the narrative of a digital divide is a false narrative and saying that Black people are not equipped for the technical industry is also a lie. The technical industry has, at its core, the major contribution of Black innovation. You cannot divorce yourself from the real genesis of ideation. So, when I see technology companies with low numbers of Black people in technical and management roles, it is clear to me that they are willing to allow the false narrative to live and breathe within their ranks.

Why would you underutilize the resource of fertile Black minds whose forebears laid the foundation for the technical industry? If the plan is to build on others or to think differently, shouldn't you have these minds throughout your organization?

My hope as a technologist and a program manager, using communication as a venue, is that we are all on the same page (pun intended)! That by reading this chapter, you are enlightened, empowered and encouraged by the technology contributions by Black people to humankind.

I also want you to remember that no matter the background, we should celebrate our collective gains that have advanced and uplifted the human race. Remember that invention and innovation is never biased, only limited by obscurity, greed, and unequal access. Let us use this knowledge to break down barriers of inequality. Let us ensure that our workplaces, communities, schools are as diverse and inclusive as possible.

Only then can we reach our utmost potential and become an uplifting example for our children and grandchildren.

So, the next time you use paper, read a printed newspaper, turn a doorknob, stop at a red light, open the refrigerator, appreciate air conditioning or central heating, ride in an elevator, or reach for your television remote, realize that these are all contributions from Black inventors. In technology, I see the infusion of Black innovation every time I pick up my cell phone, speak into a microphone or leverage the voice over IP technology used in Zoom and Microsoft Teams, speak into a RING doorbell or sign into our gaming system. These, and countless other inventions, are outstanding examples of how innovation should be used as a tool to bridge the digital divides due to racial inequity. Please partner with me to ensure that we continue to communicate the contributions of Black people to technology. Not for grandstanding, but for you to see that there has always been a place for you in tech. The digital divide is a racially biased construct that we have to expose and obliterate!

Here's one more thing I'd like to share with you.

As a member of *Toastmasters International*, a professional organization dedicated to helping amateur speakers become polished presenters, and as a leader in the Black community within Microsoft, I often use my platform to share some of the amazing technical advancements that my people have infused into society. I am truly floored by the surprised faces I see when I share these contributions and the Aha! moments that happen when the audience (of mostly technologists) recognizes that there is a disparity. After they pick their jaws up off the floor, it starts to click that something is not right and many ask, "what can I do to share this message with others?"

Technology has always been an incredible barrier-breaker. At its core, technology is simply a vehicle to help improve the human condition as we pass on our learnings and improvements from generation to generation. Humans are ever advancing as a species. As a result, the forefathers and foremothers of innovation and ideation get overshadowed by time, commercialism and even greed.

Whether we are slave or scholar, we all have the capacity to innovate, but where does true innovation come from? They say that "necessity is the mother of invention", and I believe this is the absolute truth. Black people have used necessity to drive innovation for many generations. From the use of the papyrus plant to make paper for communications, to drums and storytelling to witness and document our perilous and beautiful condition in this country and throughout the world.

I was told a long time ago that communication is the key. As a program manager and lead of a broad team of professionals, it is one of the tools I often use to ensure that we all are on message. I leverage communication tools and meetings to keep our goals in front of the team, report our status, provide a platform to report challenges and remove barriers. All of this is necessary to make sure we remain aligned and on plan.

People leave and join the team often, so it is important that I keep regular weekly and monthly meeting rhythms, so we stay on message. Communication is the vehicle to keep new members up to speed and keep the core team moving in the same direction. I cannot overstate the value of communication, repeating those rhythms and the value of staying on message to hold the entire team together. We are a very well-oiled machine. A beautiful team.

The continent of Africa provides a great example of how critical a system of communication can be. Did you know that the papyrus plant (from which we get the word paper) was used as the core platform of the world's first advanced civilizations? The ability to write, share knowledge and plans were key for organizing these civilizations that have engineered some of the greatest structures in the world. Africa, the Kingdom of Kush, Nubia, and Egypt, had many advanced civilizations when most of the world was still hovering in the dark ages. Africans were able to share knowledge of mathematics and science and had the world's first universities. Why is this important? Communications! The key is to make sure that we stay on message and do not lose sight of the contributions of Black people to technology.

Black people who are superstars and heroes, bold and courageous and brilliant. Just like you.

Chapter 6:
OBSTACLES AND OPPORTUNITIES

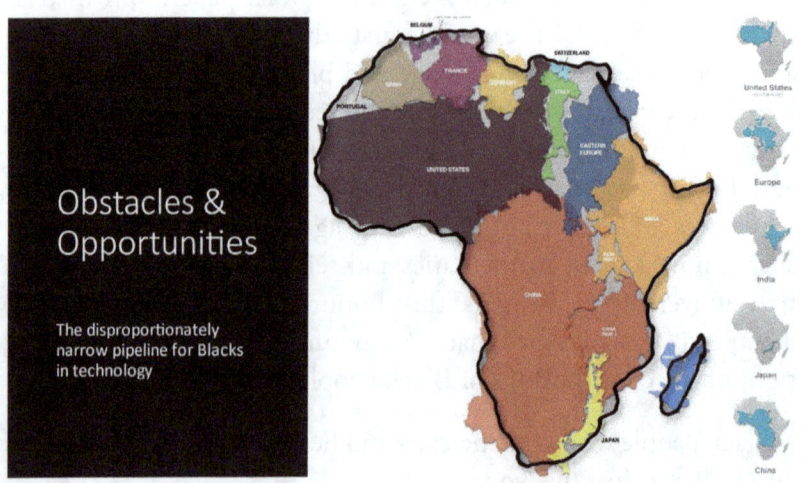

Before we dive into obstacles and opportunities, let's scope the problem and define who we are referring to when we talk about the "Black" community.

U.S. corporations tend to place all Black people into a single bucket: the African American community AND the Black community. This is no different from the buckets set out for Native American and Alaska Native, Hispanic and Latinx, Native Hawaiian and Pacific Islanders, whose numbers in tech are also low.

What makes the categorization different for my people is how large the Black and African American community is on a worldwide scale. The AAB community is really, African American/Black = Every Black person living on every continent in the world. This includes Americans, all African countries, and all Black, African, or mixed-race persons from any other country in the world that identifies as Black.

We are made to feel small, but the truth is Black people are everywhere and in vast numbers.

Take a look at any map of Africa. It is designed to appear smaller than Europe, China and even the United States. Did you know that by land mass alone, the continent of Africa could fit the entire United States, India, Europe, Britain, China, and Japan combined, with land mass left over? This includes Nigeria, Congo, and South Africa, countries whose governments share the theme of a better future for their people. Add to this, Black people across the world (including my African American lens).

Technology corporations and the United States are historically not as passionate about uplifting Black people. Make no mistake about it...I love being Black and my AAB community. I fight for our world-wide community and to uplift us every day. However, the pipeline that they are trying to fit us in is too narrow. Our community is a size 13 shoe, but this world tries to fit it into shoes that are size three, then turn around and expect us to be grateful.

In summary, technology companies are taking an entire race of people, worldwide, who have contributed to the technology that they are building their businesses on, while screening us out of technical jobs, en masse. They would like an entire race to fit into their five percent pipeline. This is not a digital divide. This, my friends, is a travesty, and we need an intervention. Let's be clear: the system has been chronically unfair, unjust, and broken for technologists who look like me.

Far too often, where there are broad opportunities offered to the privileged few, if there's a Black person in their midst, you can bet they overcame unimaginable obstacles to be in that space. Trust me, if you see a person of color in tech, especially an African American man, his story will probably be similar to mine. To reach my position, it has, and continues to be, a Herculean effort of isolation, and a hellhole of being screened out over and over, again and again and again. Every day I have to overcome the stigma of my big, Black-man box.

Microsoft's inability to "attract and retain" talent from the Black community is well documented. I would emphasize *retain* because what technologist would not want the chance to work at one of the top technology companies in the world? Blacks at Microsoft (BAM) is the Employee Resource Group (ERG) devoted to helping African American employees onboard and navigate their careers through inspiration, training and education, and community. Operating for more than 31 years, BAM is the oldest ERG at Microsoft; older than GLEAM (Gay, Lesbian, Bisexual and Transgender Employees at Microsoft), Hispanic/Latin-x, Women, Families, Military, and all other ERGs. However, Black folks have barely moved the needle in terms of landing technical, and more importantly, managerial roles in this arena.

For as long as I can remember, the number of Blacks employed at Microsoft has been limited to about four percent, and only two percent of that total work in management roles. These are the dismal numbers for Black people worldwide! Not only is it extremely difficult to get in the door at Microsoft; it can be really hard for Black people to *remain* here and even harder to grow in their careers.

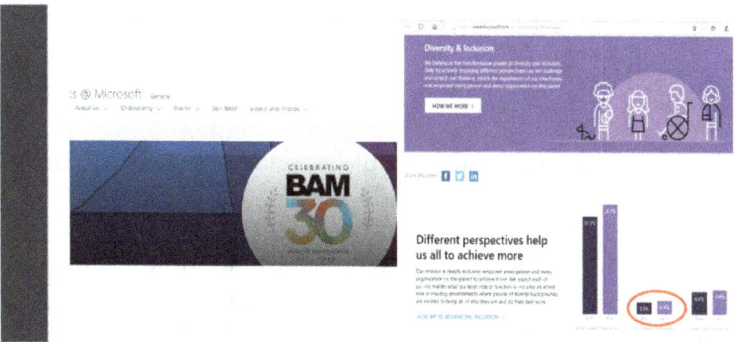

Although Blacks at Microsoft is the oldest Employee Resource Group at Microsoft, in 2018 Blacks represented only 2.4% of leaders.

In prior chapters, we have reviewed some amazing contributions to technology within the African diaspora and shown the modern-day impact of their inventions to high-tech companies. However, in companies like Microsoft, Google and Amazon, there is an ongoing struggle to "attract and retain talent." I put this term in quotes because it's a false narrative. Why? Because we are graduating more-than-capable classes of technologists every year. What technologist would not want to work for Microsoft, Google, or Amazon? Like I mentioned earlier, no one goes to college to major in computer science only to have to pivot to blue collar work!

The biggest obstacle is the systematic repression of Blacks, where corporations start with a very thin pipeline which makes it harder for Blacks to get in. Then, once they are there, the struggle continues, along with the self-doubt and the overwhelming isolation of being the only Black person on staff.

One of the hats I wear is problem manager. In this role, I perform what is called a "root cause analysis." It is a way to engineer recurring failures out of the system. Basically, I keep asking the question *why* until I get to the cause of an incident or systems outage. Then I design people, process, or technology fixes to address the root cause.

Let's use the **5 Whys** to better understand the root cause of the digital divide.

Problem Statement: Black people are not being hired and retained which creates a digital divide.

Why? #1: The culture in these companies cater to the dominant demographic of White and Asian (i.e., Indian, Chinese, Japanese and other).

Why? #2: Because of access, wealth, organization and privilege, these groups have asserted themselves as the leaders in the technical industry and created the false narrative that others don't belong.

Why? #3: Because access to capital and networks, organizations (governments/culture) and privilege are tribal; this leads to the hiring of others who look, talk, and think like you in perpetuity, to the detriment and exclusion of everyone else.

Why? #4: This has left cultures without equal access to resources, or the ability to organize in a meaningful way. Therefore Black, and African American, Native American, Hispanic and Latinx have no real chance of catching up.

Why? #5: Because the wealth, focus and pace of these companies is all about growth and forward momentum in order to take and build on other's ideas and keep it moving. This does not provide you a seat on the train. There is minimum commitment to understanding why so many folks are being left behind, and, as a result, we have a digital divide. The train has moved on and you are left at the station.

Since Black people have invented so much of the technology fundamental to the success of these top companies, the idea of "Think Different" and building on the achievements of others is, in my opinion, sinister. It means that what was another's creation is now mine where I use my access, my wealth, and my power to become even wealthier and to obfuscate any evidence of the creation not being my own! Where I come from, we call that being jacked. RIP Deebo (fyi he was the bully in the movie *Friday*)!

There are also other factors. African American innovators work in a systemically repressive society. If these same inventions were created by Asians, Nigerians or White Americans, their names would be as well-known as Bill Gates or Satya Nadella. America has done a poor job of making sure that *all* citizens have access to the high-paying technical industry. Companies veil this truth by throwing up their hands and saying, 'you cannot find the technical skills in this country.' As a result, they have all but boxed out and/or under tapped a rich source of innovation, Black people, who have proven to be fundamental to technical growth and innovation.

How are corporations addressing the digital divide that affects and impacts Black people? It's by lumping our challenges in with the broader corporate diversity and inclusion agenda. For example: BAM is just one group in a large cadre of D&I ERGs (i.e., Hispanics/Latinx, GLEAM, Women, Families, Military, etc.). You get it! These groups are a way for smaller communities to organize and to be heard. The challenge is that these particular ERGs perpetuate the same ingrained patterns. The ERGs with better access to leadership and networks, organization, and privilege, tend to do better than the ones that do not have the same access.

For example, there have been two recent changes in my organization's structure. The BAM leaders were moved to another department, and we had to start from scratch, rebuilding the new BAM team. There was a second organization change; one of our new leaders was moved out as part of that new configuration, and a second leader lost his job. So, the net result: because our numbers are so low, we feel the impact of the constant changes more than most. This traps us in a perpetual loop of storming, forming, norming and transforming.

Top of mind for me are the names of ten core members of the BAM team who have moved on in the last two years, diluting our ability to organize and affect change.

Now let's look at an example of a prospering ERG. I have selected the Women's ERG (a strong ally of the BAM community). One of Satya's greatest attributes (and this company's) is that he genuinely wants to make the world a better place. Admittedly, early in his tenure, he publicly underestimated the power of women and their ability to organize and speak truth to power. At that time, he didn't understand the challenges that women faced in the workplace. But he learned from this misstep.

Today the numbers for women in Microsoft are the best ever! Some organizations are up to 50% women, and there is a woman in what is known as the C suite (CVP, CIO, etc.) in every organization at Microsoft! This very powerful ERG was able to invoke real change. The opportunity is there for the BAM team to experience the same forward movement, but what is it going to take?

Let me wrap things up by sharing three of my experiences working to help my people gain access in the tech field. In 2018, I was invited to represent my company at *Afrotech* in San Francisco, an event that includes a huge job fair with talent flying in from all over the world to meet with top companies. I'm a people person, so I was quite excited about the opportunity to meet and talk to Black people who might want to work for a company like mine.

Afrotech Conference in San Francisco 2018

Microsoft had purchased the biggest floor presence there. All the top companies were in attendance: Google, Amazon, even Tinder, looking for young talent. The place was electric with excitement. The line to talk to Microsoft's Black technical professionals was ridiculously long. We spared no expense; we gave away t-shirts, gift bags full of tech trinkets, and we even had exclusive tickets to an after-set where we'd invite candidates who really made an impression on us!

One of the first things I noted was the company with the big G in the name was making hires on the spot. In our prep meetings, there was no discussion about available roles. We were given a talk-track that had nothing to do with onboarding. As we met people that morning, we had laptops with a few roles that they could apply for, but this did not sit well with me since we were channeling hundreds of candidates into five or so generic roles. As I started making contact, I wanted to connect further so I pulled out my own laptop and started searching for roles alongside the candidates. I personally referred at least twenty attendees with the hashtag *#Afrotech*2018. The agreement was that they would be reviewed in an elevated manner and that a recruiter would contact each one of them. This was an epic failure.

Our company had the largest presence with hundreds of candidates screened but zero hires from my team. I continued to work with the young people, making referrals, sending introductions to hiring managers, but I failed each and every one of them. I am so sorry. If I had the power and influence, I would have hired all of them.

The second case study. I attended the National Society of Black Engineers convention (NSBE) in Detroit, MI in 2019. This took place in another huge convention center. We had brought back the lessons learned from *Afrotech*, and there was serious commitment to have actual jobs in which to place people. I felt so much better about this conference. We had six months to plan, leadership was brought in, and our Global Talent team was engaged. (There was talk about taking me through training so I could make hiring decisions on site, but that did not happen).

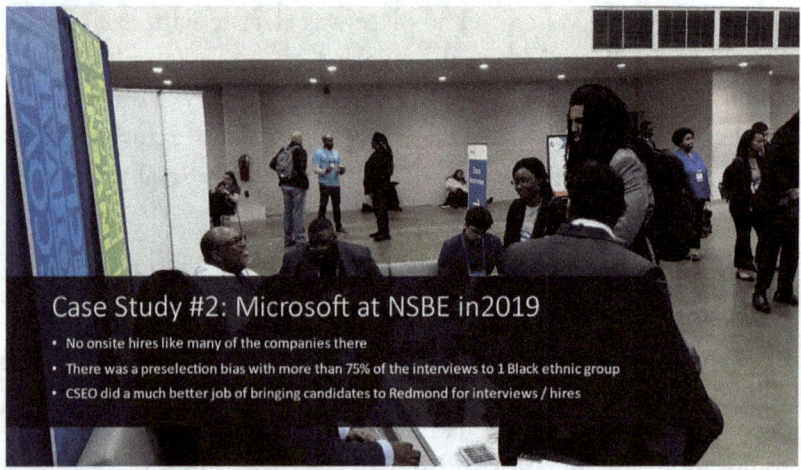

National Society of Black Engineers conference in Detroit 2019

Anyway, this venue was different. We had two separate presences. One venue was similar to our presence at *Afrotech* where potential candidates could stand in a line to talk to someone from my company, and possibly apply. If we found a rock star, they could be brought to where I was working. At the second venue where I was serving, NSBE attendees had already been prequalified and preselected for interview screenings. Those who screened well would be brought back to Redmond for face-to-face interviews. This was a much better plan that really did produce hires. I am so grateful for my leadership and the recruiting team. Where things fell short was in the selection of the candidates.

Apparently, the recruiter preselected candidates (conservatively 75%) from his nationality. I felt that our corporation and all those who worked so hard to plan this event, were being set up. This time not from outside my community, but from someone *inside* my community in a position of high trust.

To make matters worse, fifteen percent of the next candidates were Indian, leaving only less than ten percent of interviews available for our intended target, the African American and Black community. Why is this a problem? We have to consider the worldwide AAB community first, even over our national interest. I am okay with looking out for your own and maybe using your influence to carve out 15% to make sure your community is represented, but to have more than 75% of the interviewees from one African country in a global talent event is an abuse of power, poor stewardship of the company's resources and a total disregard of the efforts of so many people to make the event successful. It displayed a real lack of empathy for the pain of the entire African American and Black community.

Another significant challenge with the screening process: there are online tools and software that you can practice with to prepare you for a technical interview. I believe that many of the candidates who had advance notifications had practiced and prepared. Candidates who showed up, and did well, had access to very specific internet tools to help them. All the Indian candidates and one African American candidate had taken advantage of the right preparation tools. Of course, many of the candidates from the highly represented nationality had access as well. I found that this method of screening out was unfairly blocking great talent. The remaining candidates were trying to prepare based on four to six years of education and did not show up as well.

We need to offer prep guidance for technical interviews so EVERYONE who puts in the time will have the same opportunity to prepare well. Although the numbers were skewed and my group was not able to do onsite hiring like many of the companies there (and the numbers were heavily skewed to one nationality), our team did a much better job bringing candidates to main campus for a day of interviewing, and we made a good number of hires.

What we can learn from this is that *what* we did was a great thing, but *how* it was executed was lacking. Although I am African American, I try not to incorporate bias into any of my BAM work. To see that recruiter who preselected candidates in such a partial manner, for what could have been such a wonderful opportunity for Black conference attendees, really saddened me.

The last case study really hit home. One Sunday my director reached out to me. I am not calling her by name, but she is a beautiful person from the inside out who really cares about her employees and puts her heart into her work. I don't even remember the national injustice making the news at the time. It may have been Travon Martin. Anyway, my director reached out to me because she wanted to post something on *Yammer* (a Microsoft product and our internal social media tool) to shed light on the pain in the Black community. She asked for my opinion, and I told her that I thought it was fine to post it, but to be careful. Sometimes, if you are too "pro Black," you will become the target. I did not want her to experience that.

From that email dialogue, I committed to strengthening my efforts to support our community. I started a BAM chapter for my local team and developed our strategy and plan, one of which was to fast-track Black hires to fill open roles. We were all obviously great hires. Surely each of us knows somebody in tech who would be a great fit for the company.

I asked all of my fellow BAM chapter leads to provide ten resumes each. Not just anyone, but people who had something to offer. We gathered a pool of over fifty individuals, some of whom were prior technical execs. The list consisted of folks with master's and doctorate degrees and some college hires. From there I worked with leadership, human resources, and our global talent teams to build a screening process to begin placing candidates in open roles in our organization. Using the in-place processes, we landed zero interviews!

It was not the talent. It was the system, the process, and the managers.

Landing zero interviews for PhDs, former IBM executives, and master's in computer science candidates in a program sponsored by one of the world's greatest tech companies, still blows my mind! Some of those candidates were my friends and some were my family. Even my own children, so this became very personal to me. This, and a few other unfortunate events, caused me to resign my position in BAM, just for a season. (I told you that I never give up).

Of my original list of ten candidates who were not able to get an interview through the organized program, three are Microsoft full time employees today, and I am working on one more. I will not quit until all those that I promised I would work for, are in.

What is very wrong with this picture? I am able to hustle and find a way to get one or two people in the door through my individual efforts, but even with leadership support and as a BAM leader, I could not get the system to offer a single interview.

But please don't misread my intent for this chapter. There is lots and lots of hope. Every November, Microsoft publishes its annual Diversity and Inclusion Report which breaks out hiring by race, gender, etc. I got a chance to watch this year's update in a Senior Leadership Team townhall live stream event. I had been keeping up with these numbers for years and for as long as I have been tracking them, they have been the same. Microsoft has 4.5% Black employees, most in non-tech roles, most working in retail with 2.4% in managerial roles. But this time I heard the leader repeat feedback that I had shared in the past, that as Microsoft tries to solve problems of social injustice, they need to take a look in the mirror to see how they are contributing to systematic repression.

I am taking a contextual liberty from the scripture First Timothy 3:5 as its intent is to qualify leaders of the church, but I believe this is really relevant to anyone in leadership. Paraphrased, it states: your ministry starts at home. How can you serve the world, and your house is not in order? On the corporate or societal level, how can our company do great philanthropic things to uplift the world when someone under our leadership is being oppressed?

On October 21, 2021, Lindsay-Rae McIntyre, Microsoft's CVP Chief Diversity Officer, shared the 2021 Diversity and Inclusion report (http://aka.ms/DIReport) numbers: 5.7% for AAB 3.9% for managers, and across the board, numbers were up in technical and even director and executive roles. Wait, what? We are being heard and the numbers don't lie! This was the most positive movement for the AAB community that I have seen in my eighteen years at Microsoft. But she did not stop there.

When people present goals, I listen for the 5-letter acronym, SMART (Specific, Measurable, Actionable, Realistic and Time-bound). McIntyre said that Microsoft's SLT has a committed goal of doubling the number of Black and Hispanic managers and executive managers by 2025. I was blown away. This is by no means the endgame, but we are off to a great start. I am so hopeful that the AAB community will at least, through Microsoft, be able to realize their technical dreams and participate fully and abundantly in the current technical boom. The results are real, and the numbers do not lie!

A Black Journey in Tech

We are making progress. See for yourself.

Chapter 7:
UNDERSTANDING CHANGE

I shared this speech in a 2020 regional *Toastmasters* competition.

Connecting You to Everyone and Everything Ever

By Dwight D. Jones

"I'd like to show you how we are kindred to the smallest particles and at the same time have commonality with the farthest reaches of the universe. I am going to connect all of us all the way back to the very beginning of time, through the present, to the absolute very end. What's even more amazing is that what I am about to reveal to you, you are already intimately familiar with. It's as constant to us as our own heartbeat. Are you ready, for this profound revelation? ARE YOU READY?

At the nucleus of everything ever is change! Yes, that's right, change. It is the common denominator that binds us together, connecting you to everyone and everything ever! Animal, plant, mineral or other. It is the constant that unites us across time and space. Change is the vehicle that proclaims because you exist, you will always exist, you will just "change". Whether you believe in the big bang or that God spoke, you were there, unaware but traveling through time and space until the present day. But not just you, everything brought into existence has been and is on the exact same journey. Today, like caterpillars, we live our lives busy as ever, until one day we tuck away into our cocoons and it's over...or so we think. Imagine with me, if you will, *a shared end or a new beginning where we all spring forward, reshaped into beautiful butterflies designed by the physics of change.*

So, you see, change is a constant and we must adapt to it. How well and how much change we can manage will determine not only the quality, but also the quantity of our lives. Change does not discriminate. It can be good or bad, permanent, or temporary, expected or catch us totally off guard. It is the base requirement for every organism. From the highest king to the unemployed or impoverished, we cannot lose ourselves from the responsibility of change. Every idea, plan, improvement, construct, or inspiration has at its root, change.

Change has a repeatable pattern: from change (something made different) to chaos (disruption, disorder, and confusion) to control (manage, restrain or limit), then back to change again. Natural, expected, planned, seamless, or managed, positive change is the highest ideal. The more that we have, the more added change we can manage.

At its opposite end is abrupt, impactful, unexpected change that yields a negative result. This is the worst type of change, costing us dearly and quite difficult to recover from. Taking a sip of water is me managing change. Having the glass of water unexpectedly poured on my head is unexpected change.

Think of the example we are all living with today: the Corona virus. This is the worst kind of change. Here is my explanation of the patterns of change:

Change - Something was made different – The virus was released on the human population

Chaos – Disruption, disorder, and confusion

Control – We are desperately trying to manage, restrain and limit

I am sure that together we will survive, but the world will never be the same as a result of this devastating pandemic.

I believe that the ultimate outcome of change will be positive, regardless of how we get to this shared end. The one thing that is certain is that we will all get there together because we are eternally connected by change."

I shared this speech with you to open your eyes to the significant role that change plays in the life of a technologist. We must be flexible and stay ahead of it. Actually, one of my Dwightisms (key lessons from my experience; see the next chapter for a fuller explanation) is "change! See the bigger picture!" This is so profound and fundamental that it's worthy of its own chapter.

I had initially named this paragraph *Conquering Change*. What a joke! No one conquers change. The best we can do is try to understand it, know where we are based on the patterns of change, chaos, and control, and do our best to manage from there. We must reconcile the fact that we cannot divorce ourselves from change. We are all bound to each other by change, and here are our choices: we can just let what is going to happen *happen* and be the surprised victim of the result, or we can expect it, understand the patterns, and do our best to plan, take change head on, and make peace with the (hopefully)better results.

I have many examples of having to face change head on. When I first started out as a technologist, I soon learned to expect some type of major change every three to five years. For example, change number one: my company downsized, and I was totally unprepared. This threw me out of tech and had me washing cars for a living!

My pastor used to say the first time the dog bites you, it's on the dog. The second time, it's on you. This was the same pastor who counseled me to get back into technology.

After about four years in my next job at Decatur Federal Savings & Loans, we went through a huge restructuring and downsizing. I did not want to live through another morale drain, watching my friends being laid off and waking up each morning wondering if I was next on the list. This time I used the skills I'd gained and took another job to avoid going down with the ship. This launched me into an even better opportunity, and it all stemmed from this initial lesson learned from *change*. I firmly believe that not understanding the demands of change (and not being willing to go with the flow of change) in technology is the downfall of many tech newbies.

Think about it. The jobs that most of us have in college (like when I worked for KFC and McDonalds, or as a security guard, game floor host, or in a warehouse) were all built on the same premise; you come to work, you follow the routine, and you get paid. I am sure this is the mindset of professions like banking, pharmacy, teaching, etc. Whether you work a white or a blue-collar job, you have to deal with change, but usually it's in the confines of a well-defined work structure where you can find solace in rhythms and routine.

In the high technology field, however, change can happen monthly. As a technologist, you have to become comfortable with totally reinventing yourself every two to four years. Otherwise, you may need to consider another field. A degree is not enough. There is no sitting back in technology. You have to think like a lifelong learner or you will become as obsolete as the Cabbage Patch (a dance we used to do in high school when the deejay played anything by Parliament Funkadelic).

In the last twelve months, my department has been through four reorganizations. Most of these I don't feel, but each reorganization has wreaked havoc on our local BAM program.

One tool I've used to stay current is to gain professional certifications. It's helped me move from earning $50k a year (which was a lot in the 90's) ☺ to a $100k consultant, which was also a lot in the 90's.

For me, it started with Microsoft Career Certifications. I passed a few exams and became a certified Microsoft Career Professional, then I added the Internet Professional to that, then I finally completed the major one at the time and became a Microsoft Certified Systems Engineer. For most of my technical certification, I did not have the money or time for classes, but the demand from companies looking for the skills, and the money and the mouths I had to feed were motivation enough.

I was able to go to my local bookstore and buy the courseware and/or the exam cram study guides. I would put the children to bed, take a brief rest, wake up and study from three to five am, then go back to bed and be up for work by 7am. This was my routine until I took, and passed, the test sometimes after multiple failures, which is also part of the process.

Guess what though? I remained relevant and with every certification test I passed, I saw increases in pay and opportunity. I expanded beyond my Microsoft certifications with Cisco Career Certifications. This made me a technical expert not only with Microsoft Server and Client platforms, but also with the networking. I passed all the Cisco Certification exams that I could afford. I was a certified Design Associate, Network Associate, Network Professional, Design Professional, and I even passed the written portion of the internetworking exam which was the top professional certification at the time.

How did staying ahead of the pace of technical change help? I told you that I doubled my salary. I also became very much in demand. Understanding that I needed to be a lifelong learner, and stay a few steps ahead of technology, paid major dividends.

I can remember when I was being interviewed for a networking job at Bell South Internet Services. This was my first opportunity to land a hands-on role. I had made it through the manager's interview, and I remember our core team lead came to conduct the technical interview. Without going into detail, he asked me complex questions about building a highly available network design. I was able to draw one out on the whiteboard because it was on the CCDA exam I'd had passed the week before, and the rest is history. I got the job and had never even logged onto a router or switch. Hey, I was dictating changes instead of reacting. What a noble concept!

Another huge adaptation you must make when you work for a hi-tech company is that you have to write your story, communicate your value and impact, and have it stand up against others in your organization. This was another huge lesson for me.

For every other company that I worked for, receiving an annual review or evaluation went something like this: the manager had a breakout of the functions of your job and there was some sort of rating system to determine whether you were excelling, on par, or needed improvement along with some type of comment box. It does not work that way at Microsoft.

As the employee, you must set your core priorities, you have to track your progress toward goals, and you have to show your own value based on what you delivered and your impact on other's success. As the often-quoted poem "Invictus" states, "I am the captain of my fate, I am the master of my soul!" If your motivation is to advance in pay and position, you must master this responsibility. Of course, Microsoft has tools and training to help with this, but this is key.

Change. See the bigger picture! This hit me like a Mack truck. One of the subtle and career-limiting expectations that I had in common with many who are new to the field is that we want to be seen and recognized for what we have done in an industry that really only recognizes forward momentum. This can be very difficult for Black people when we have worked so hard to obtain a degree or a position of status.

When you walk in a room with my colleagues, none of that is ever mentioned. We are too busy trying to pioneer the technology of the future. It is a general assumption that if you are in the room, you are smart, and what we need is for you to bring your best self, your authentic self, lean in and add value to the collective team. We are patient and if you are new, you will be given every opportunity to grow, but you must be self-motivated, curious, and driven. It's really up to you to prove that you *don't* fit in or *don't* belong. Disengagement is the fast track to proving that.

I also want you to understand that feedback is a gift. Changing yourself and your behavior doesn't happen overnight. It takes effort and time to develop and perfect the skills that will take you to the next level, therefore you have to be open to receiving feedback. It's not an affront to who you are, and you should never become defensive, even if you do not agree. Just say "thank you for the feedback" and let it go. We all have blind spots, and I would rather someone tell me I have a booger in my nose, than to think I'm clean and ready to give the perfect presentation.

Speaking of presentations, I delivered one in front of Tony Scott, Microsoft's CIO at the time. After the presentation, I was on a high. I was being complimented by members of the leadership team and told that my message was delivered in a consumable way, and that real action would surely be the outcome.

When I got back to my office, I had an unprompted email from the only Black Partner Director in the room, Mario Pipkin. Now I knew of Mario, but I had never met him personally. He had taken time to record about 20 seconds of my speech, and he said simply, "good presentation; you need to work on your umms and *ands*."

I read the email and for about a half second, my defensive mechanism was about to kick in: "bro I nailed it. Why can't you ride with that?" But I had the example right there on file, and I knew he was right. I used "umm" and "you know" so much, and I also had a manager who only wanted bold and brief conversations. I can hear Tom now: "Dwight, tell me in ten words or less."

Well, I am from the South, and everything is a story. Anyway, this invaluable feedback led me to *Toastmasters*, an international speaking organization that has moved me from stuttering to writing and delivering award-winning speeches.

Mario is still my coach today. He retired from Microsoft several years back as the company's first Black Partner Director. He was a trusted advisor and led many programs for Bill Gates. If you get to know Mario, you will soon understand that he's THE model of changing and seeing the bigger picture. You see, back in the day, he was "straight hood" and a "banger," but he was smart and redirected himself onto a totally different track.

My Brother has a degree from the Art Institute, which is not a knock. The way he can visualize, layout and communicate ideas is beyond genius. It's on a savant level. He came to Microsoft as a developer and catapulted himself to one of the highest positions a Black person has held in Microsoft Digital. Mario, to this day, wears braids, long fingernails...everything that says *real* in the urban community. However, without flipping a switch, covering, or changing his authenticity, he can carry a room where he might be the only person of color.

He shared with me that it was not always that way. When his coach had to show him that he was too rough around the edges and that people were afraid of him, he took that feedback and adjusted for it. Now the brother is untouchable. When he retired, Microsoft lost an Icon. If we had a Hall of Fame, Mario would definitely have his own plaque hanging on the wall.

At Microsoft, it is all about accelerating capabilities. How do we get to market faster? Experiment, fail fast, learn, and grow. There is very little time to stop and smell the flowers. This type of climate can be very disheartening, especially, since in other professions, advancement may be based on education, tenure, or status.

We all desire to be seen and recognized, and for Black people, it is overdue. However, the higher you get in technology, you'll find that up-leveling and promotions become fewer and far between. It took me seventeen years to move from level 60 to Principal, five levels! Microsoft employees can reach level 80 and beyond, but at this point in my career, reaching those aspirational echelons are a pipe dream for me. Hopefully I am paving the way for some of you to become level 80 and above. Wouldn't that be wonderful?

How did my up-leveling journey look in practicality? I have always been a top performer. That's why I received four promotions in five years in my first tech job, followed by my next job and after about a year, being promoted there. That is where I transitioned into a lead/management role where I continued to advance but eventually hit my first plateau. There was no additional upward mobility in the mid-sized corporate construct I was in. That's when I moved to consulting and made technical leaps that landed me at Microsoft.

At Microsoft, I took a role that, based on my industry skills and experience, was under my true level. After all, I was a Cisco Certified Internetwork Expert*, a former Senior Systems Architect delivering the first Windows design for Bank of America, and I'd moved from that to a core team network engineer for BellSouth Internet Services. Why did I take the job? The money was a nearly $40k increase from what I was making, plus there was a bonus to relocate, and they offered a man with a wife and six children a deal that even my current CIO agreed I should accept.

Starting in a lower role to get my foot in the door also gave me an opportunity to learn the inner workings of a company on a scale unlike anything I'd experienced before, and to use that industry experience to shine. Boy did I shine! I loved, loved, loved my job, my team, my managers, everything about working in MSN Global Network Services. This was the first time my work, ideation and innovation were not stymied and did not have to be represented by a consulting company or "superior."

I wrote the process for standardizing a portion of the network platform, and I deployed the first global network automation tool used by Microsoft. I was promoted, received a very secretive Gold Star Stock Award, other industry awards, and because I was trusted and valued in my role, I always got to work on the coolest stuff. I was loved by our Corporate Vice President (Deborah Chrapaty). She actually funded me to bring the entire senior high school class of young ladies from Southwest Atlanta Christian Academy to stay in Redmond for a week to participate in the *Digigirlz* technology camp.

The last example of how change forced me to see the bigger picture really comes out a place of pain, anxiety, and depression. I touch on this in the article I wrote "Never Give Up!" in the chapter titled the same.

I read in a book somewhere, "what got you here, will not get you there." I will share that nugget for free. It is absolutely true. Moving up in Microsoft beyond the MSN years came with lots more pressure, responsibility and even failure. I was happy with my recent paygrade promotion and the MSN team, but I knew that I was still under-leveled, and I was searching for opportunities to prove it. I thought I had found my chance to prove myself in a Senior Engagement Manager role for the now defunct Microsoft TV program supporting my former employer, Bell South. This role was posted as a level 63/64 role, and I had just been promoted to level 61. I had all of the skills and landed the job, but company policy would not allow them to move me up again after just receiving a promotion. The verbal agreement we reached was that every six months they would look at moving me to the next level.

Well, on day one I received all of the work and pressure that comes with being a Senior Engagement Manager for a customer-facing account. The customer was not very happy because Bellsouth was being bought out by AT&T, and they were using Microsoft's *Media Room* platform as the underlying content delivery platform for AT&T U-verse to the detriment of BellSouth.

This was the first job where I thought that I would die from the stress. Nevertheless, I took a $50k account and rebooted it into a $460M account for Microsoft, and my portion of if brought 48% margins. Not bad for a level 61, right? Promotion's coming right? Wrong. I don't know if it was my direct manager or the entire organization, but this was the worst division that I had worked in at Microsoft. My manager did not care if the VPs at BellSouth cursed me out on the daily and called me everything that a White, empowered, and angry man in the South could think of.

I never received a poor review, but I was never up-leveled and my review conversations were the bare minimum, with me getting my annual raise on a posted note in the airport. What made matters worse was my job was subversively moved from Atlanta to Texas and even after the hard work, I was told my position was being eliminated, and that I had 30 days to find another job in Microsoft or I would be terminated! I was under so much stress and pressure that I could not see a way out. This was during the housing market collapse, so I was living in a house that was undervalued, I was dealing with an external legal challenge and now I was about to be laid off!

I thank God for His grace and mercy. An angel, a Black man named David Meachum who was a director for Microsoft IT Windows Services, told me "Nah, I am not going to let them do that to you. Come work for me." His generosity brought me to the group I'm in today, Microsoft Digital.

Talk about unplanned change! The job on David's team required me to relocate back to Redmond. My family needed to stay put in Georgia because my wife was working full time, the children were settled in school and there was no way to sell our home. The position was a level 61, the exact same level I had when I was working in MSN. On top of this, I had to find an apartment to live in with my family nearly 3,000 miles away. This change took me down a very dark path with no exits in sight. I was hurt, angry, afraid, and alone.

Although I was grateful for the role, continuing my career so that I could provide for my family, the emotional pressure I was under and doing my best to compartmentalize, was completely overwhelming. Every day at work was a struggle. I was functioning well and never had a poor review, but I'd lost the passion to be the top performer. I'd been knocked all the way back to that place I remembered from my childhood, once again a ship without a rudder, sail, or compass. I felt invisible and unremarkable, destined for last place in my career. Returning to Redmond, I had no friends, no one to talk to outside of work, and I felt invisible in the mostly White church I attended. I did my best to work hard and exercise, but most of my evenings ended with me bench pressing a bottle of Jack Daniels.

It all came crashing down on me one night. I woke up with my heart racing. I could hear the dog in the apartment above, and it felt like he was crying for me. I had my first panic attack. I thought I was having a heart attack and that I was going to die. I was in shambles; my marriage was on the rocks. I was working at Microsoft in the day and *UPS* at night to make ends meet. I didn't even know how to ask for help. Someone please throw me a lifeline!

After nearly two years of this torture, my wife and I made one of the most important decisions of our lives. We decided to fight for our marriage, find a place to live, and relocate our family back to Redmond. This meant that I had to let the house I had purchased in 1996 go to foreclosure. My credit was ruined, my wife and I were wounded, but we were together. But it's always darkest just before the dawn. The sun's light came in; I had my family back together again and, through the process, we found counseling.

I had never thought about marital counseling outside of my church in Atlanta, but *Microsoft Cares* is a free confidential counselling service available to all employees, and it was there for me when I needed it most. If you are a Microsoft Employee and have access to it, use it. For anyone else, if you are in a dark place, please reach out for help. Getting help changed my paradigm, which changed my life.

My wife and I were in couple's therapy, and for the first time in my life, I had secular counseling. These sessions allowed me to really get to the bottom of some of the challenges I had growing up and being a Black person in tech. It allowed me a space within which it was okay to be heard and to determine what was best for me. I had spent a lifetime putting everything and everyone ahead of me. One counseling revelation that became my mantra: change and see the bigger picture.

My fuse was relit. I found my passion for technology again. I made a conscious decision to change from bitter to better. The results were without question. I went from making average performance scores to top performance scores. I was promoted to Senior Service Engineering Manager; I won the individual CIO award in 2013 which was the top MSIT award at the time. This placed me on the road to Principal that I'm still on today.

In the next chapter, *Dwightisms*, I will share with you a few tools to add to your kit. My hope is that you will learn and leverage to avoid some of my mistakes. You totally have my permission to build on my experiences. Take these lessons and fly higher and further than I could only dream of. Really, that is what this is all about; honoring the path laid for me by my mother's mothers and father's fathers and all those souls who sacrificed so much to provide the opportunities I have today. I pray that my ancestors are proud of how I did not accept the narrative that had been written for me.

I chose to change and see the bigger picture. If I can do it, so can you.

Chapter 8:
DWIGHTISMS

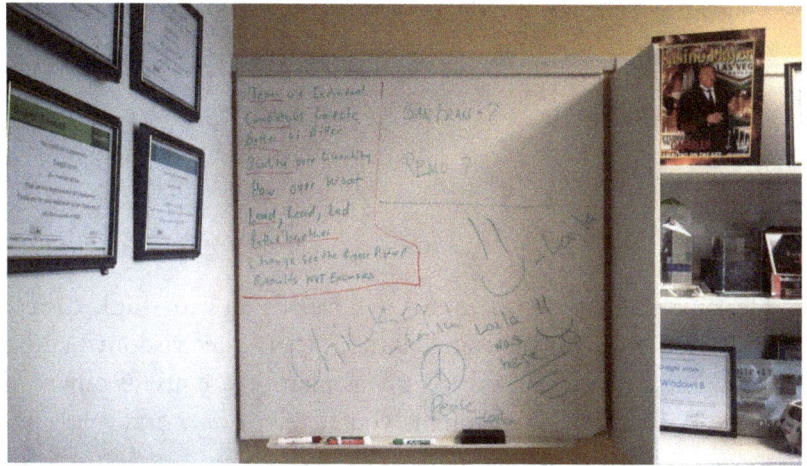

I keep my key lessons learned (Dwightisms) on my whiteboard in my office

I have always been fascinated by the power of sayings. I love how tiny bites of wisdom can be condensed down into catchy, easily remembered snippets that can save your life or at least make you wiser. What makes these sayings so amazing is that they are time-honored, harkening to the era in which they were created, but years later, the meanings still hold the same weight.

I grew up hearing these 'turn of phrases' bouncing freely from person to person. My family was only a generation or two from slavery, so there were tons of life-affirming aphorisms exchanged between folks who understood the power of words. Actually, these words of wisdom became part of America's fabric. A few that come to mind are:

A penny saved is a penny earned

Don't look a gift horse in the mouth

A stitch in time saves nine

A bird in the hand is worth two in the bush

The early bird catches the worm

A day late and a dollar short

Red on yellow kill a fellow. Red on black is a friend of Jack

Hindsight is 20/20

Measure twice, cut once

Walk soft, but carry a big stick

Hearing these time-tested sayings caused me to think deeper about what the words meant, and to apply the wisdom behind them. The ones created during my generation are just as powerful but are not as fun. We brought you *stranger danger* and *stop, drop, and roll (*which you need to remember if you're on fire, but it's not quite as fun as the old folks' sayings).

When I was a child, my mother and father, who were born in the 1920s, would repeat little truisms of warning, wisdom, and guidance. Some were funny and playful, but I knew that if I took time to go a little bit deeper, the meanings would save me tons of pain and anguish. Here are a few of them:

A hard head will make a soft behind

A word to the wise should be sufficient

Don't take any wooden nickels

Pride comes before the fall

If you make your bed hard, you are the one that will have to lie in it

Never bite the hand that feeds you

One that my mother came up with in 2021 as we were talking about Psalms chapter 1 – *You see the tree and you see the fruit, but do you know the root?*

Now, I did not have that much time with my dad and most of my lessons from him were through observations, but the things he taught me were poignant and locked in my heart. Please allow me to stretch past the tiny snippet rule as I honor my father.

"Son, I don't care if you become a street sweeper, but be the best street sweeper you can be." Note: The street sweepers he is referring to are the men who followed horses and buggies around.

"You are not better or worse than anyone. All people are the same."

"You can learn from everyone. Learn from and be willing to listen to everyone, even if it is someone poorer than you, you can learn from them."

"There are two sides to every story."

"Two wrongs don't make a right."

In the mid-1970s, my father taught me an important lesson about words and empathy. Up to that point, I'd been raised mostly by my mother and siblings. We were at church multiple times a week, and I knew church etiquette. I viewed the world through the lens of a southern Baptist kid.

My brothers took me to visit my father who was handling some trucking business in the D.C. area. One day during the visit, there was lots of snow on the ground. I remember riding around and, at one point, I noticed prostitutes standing on the corner wearing miniskirts in the freezing cold. I was probably eight or nine years old, and I can't remember exactly what I said, but it was something like "look at those bad ladies."

This is when my father took the time, not in a scolding tone, but in a teachable manner, to explain something to me that I can appreciate to this day. This man, who was known for being hard, terse, and no-nonsense, was always gentle with me. He patiently explained "that you don't know why those ladies are out there. Some of them may be mothers with mouths to feed and doing what they are doing is the only way they could eat." This was profound and eye-opening, and it immediately kicked the knees out from under the high horse that I rode in on and instilled a sense of empathy that I carry to this day. This may not seem like much to you but being able to see all people under the same tent and making room in your heart for different perspectives is a supreme gift. Thank you, dad.

Those words of wisdom, my Christian upbringing, and my journey as a technical professional, have also provided me with my own set of sayings and guidance that I share with those I mentor. Some may not be unique, but they were new to me when I first encountered them.

I keep most of these treasures on a whiteboard in my office so that I can always refer to them for myself and my mentees. I will spend the remainder of this chapter listing them out, sharing context and a brief explanation.

Dwightisms

1. I developed a really clear formula for instructing job candidates on how to do well in interviews: Success = (Attitude + Technical Ability) X Hours Applied or (SAT)H – One of my most dear friends and brothers in this world is Srinath "Sunny" Duddilla. Sunny is the founder and president of SunPlus Data Group Inc. SunPlus is a software development

and consulting company in Atlanta. Early in my consulting career, Sunny betted on me and invested in my success. I was a consultant through his company when I landed roles with Norfolk Southern Railway and BellSouth Internet Services. When I was not actively consulting, I worked as an account manager, helping to place other consultants into technical roles. Most of his employees were from India, and SunPlus was their U.S. H1B visa sponsor. I was instrumental in helping the consultants, who were new to America, transition into US culture and prepare for their first roles.

I learned so much from working with Sunny, and it really helped me to overcome a lot of the fears associated with interviews and the interviewing process. That is when I discovered (SAT)H. One of the main problems that we were having when we sent candidates out for job interviews was our candidate's inability to connect with the American hiring managers. Our candidates were on edge and nervous, there were huge communications gaps, and they would lose the opportunity. What I told these candidates was that every job is a new adventure and that most communication is non-verbal anyway. I helped them relax when I showed them that no one understands anyone 100%. Even with someone as close as a spouse or best friend, communication is never really without issue. Ask my wife!

In addition, rarely does someone have all of the skills to win a job, but if the interviewer can see you as a highly motivated, likable person who is willing to learn, the fact that you made it to the interview means you have a very decent shot of landing the job. Technical skills can be taught and learned. Who teaches the class on how to be President? No one; you win the election, and you learn on the go. Right?

I was able to demonstrate this when I landed the job for BellSouth Internet Services. It was for an experienced Cisco network engineer, and I had just self-studied and passed the

CCDA and was studying for my CCNA. I went to that interview and applied (SAT)H. I was hungry and enthusiastic and willing to learn. I had no hands-on experience, but I was able to demonstrate the book knowledge I had amassed. This landed me the contract, and I grew technically by leaps and bounds. Before I left Bell South as a consultant, I was one of three on the core engineering team, and I had numerous commendations including a certificate of excellence and a plaque for outstanding job performance. I am convinced that the connection I made with the interviewers and my application of (SAT)H landed me that job and every role since.

2. Lack vs. Prosperity Model —This model came to me during my prayer time somewhere between 2005 and 2006. I was working for Microsoft in Atlanta, and I had never been out of debt. We still lived pretty much paycheck to paycheck. Credit management was not part of my life, and I accepted the false narrative of Black people and bad credit. That is when I got the revelation, laid out in the chart below, that made the complex simple. It showed me the difference between good debt and bad debt, and that over time, there was a line in the middle where I could live in prosperity. It did not happen overnight, and I had to go through many hardships, including losing my house, but I had the vision and the plan and today I own a home that is worth ten times more than the house I let go. My credit score is well over 800, and I only owe for my house and carry very little credit card debt. My children had the opportunity to attend college and what I had to pay was paid in full.

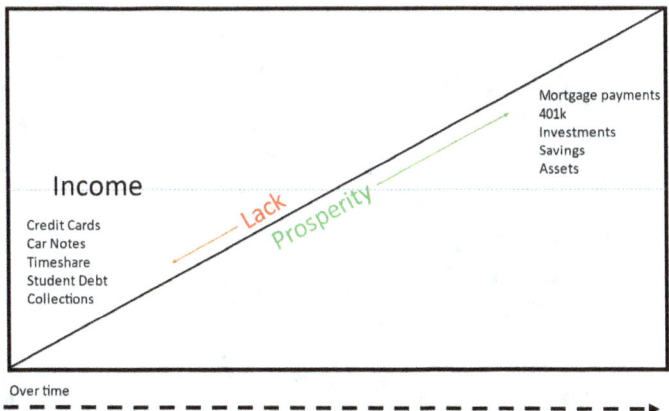

3. Lead, Led, Lead (as in heavy metal) is my use of word play for a speech I wrote where I used the words lead (verb) as in leader or leadership; led (verb) act of being directed; and lead, the heavy dense metal, to show the subtleties of leadership. The purpose of this speech was to encourage leaders to lead. Members of *Toastmasters* not only help each other improve as speakers, but we develop each other as leaders as well.

With this Dwightism, I ask the individual or group how they define leadership. I often cite examples of presidents or celebrities, military leaders or even action movie heroes. After I hear a few common examples, I share my example of leadership and I show a mother caressing her child. For me this is the prototype of leadership.

A good, loving mother will do anything for her child. There have been cases where mothers have lifted cars off of their babies or walked into flames to rescue their precious child. A mother's life is second to her babies'. She comes close to death to bring the child into the world, and from there, she spends her life nurturing that son or daughter to become something better than herself. She does this without being asked, and she expects little in return. Good mothers are the ultimate servant leaders and my case for leadership.

At this point, I get a few nods of agreement.

From there I share a case study from a training I took in which I was selected to lead a group of six individuals in a teambuilding exercise. We were competing with several other tables in the room. The participants were all blindfolded except for me. I was the moderator, overseeing their task of putting together a puzzle with different shapes and colors. It was not a complex puzzle, but they had to ask the right questions in order to solve it.

I sat at the head of the table. There were six men representing three nationalities. I will name them Group A, Group B and Group C. There were three men in Group A to my left, two men in Group B at my opposite end, and one gentleman from Group C on my right. I saw many dynamics play out across different cultures.

The first thing I observed was that the gentleman from Group C dropped a puzzle piece on the floor. It was obvious that he knew it had fallen down, he was noticeably disturbed by it, but he did not mention it. The gentlemen in Group A proceeded to inquire of all team members, including asking them to share what puzzle pieces they had and to explain them to the group. One of the Group B gentlemen chimed in and made two or three good suggestions on how the team could solve the puzzle that moved the collective group in the right direction. Then something very strange happened.

The other gentleman in Group B started interrupting and talking over the first man to the point where the first guy physically leaned back and only engaged when called upon. The team became very frustrated when they called for a count of the puzzle pieces, and they were one short. I was frustrated too and asked the gentleman from Group C, "Did a piece drop down near you?" He responded "yes," and the entire table could not believe that he held back that key piece of information.

Our table did not finish the puzzle in time, but this exercise in teaming taught me a valuable lessons in leadership that I have never forgotten. There are loud, vocal leaders who use power, money, and influence to gain their right to lead. I think of them as Boss Hog from *The Dukes of Hazzard* television show. Then there is the dynamic of being led. That was the team coming together and moving as a unit. Then there were those who disengaged and became dead weight.

I flashed a slide to show that we are all capable of leading, being led or being dead weight from disengagement. My key takeaways from this are 1. Be yourself. We are all called to lead in our own sphere. 2. Pay attention to the subtleties of leading vs participating and disengagement. If you are naturally laid back, cerebral and quiet like many people can be, especially those who have insecurities, you will have to work really hard to stay engaged 3. Do what you must do to stay engaged and 4. Realize that you make a difference, and it is noticeable when you are disengaged.

4. Results over Excuses – When I pledged my college fraternity, Kappa Alpha Psi, one of the things my line brothers and I had to commit to memory and repeat as a unit was Kappa's definition of excuses. What are excuses? "Excuses are the tools of the incompetent. They build monuments to nothingness. Those that use them seldom amount to anything." Hard words to an 18-year-old pledgee, but these iron words helped forge me into a man. They were stamped on my soul, reminding me that it is imperative to deliver what I say, and if I don't, own the failure. There really is not much in between. The business world can be super harsh. There may be more riding on you when you're meeting your deliverable or fixing a problem in a timely manner.

Very recently, I had to step in to fix a problem impacting our end-users. There was finger pointing, disengagement and procrastination, all at the end user's expense. I had to intervene and do the necessary hard work to get to the root cause of the problem, but I worked with the right teams, of course, and we very rapidly resolved the issues. I had a meeting with one of the leaders across the entire program who told me how big a deal it was that we fixed the user issues, and that he believed if we had not, our key stakeholder might have cancelled the entire program. Remember, it is okay to fail, but please own it when you do. No excuses.

5. How Over What – This to me is very key. You accomplished your goal, but did you leave a trail of bodies? Did you bring others with you on the journey? This speaks to empathy, awareness, and integrity. Is it okay to run redlights to rush someone to the hospital? This is a tough question. You have to measure your chances of getting there safely, the level of the emergency and the harm you might inflict on others. Will I cause other motorists to have accidents because of my reckless driving?

   It's really a sinking feeling when you are in a meeting with someone who is demonstrating work or a new feature, and you know that the way they accomplished the work was never really part of the plan. Yay you! But if I present and the team is with me, the leaders are informed and I am hitting well-communicated targets, then you know the *how* has been prioritized over the *what*. It may take a little longer to deliver, but the impact will be greater, with less confusion and with fewer questions.

6. Team Over Individual – One of my greatest joys growing up was playing high school football. I loved the sense of kinship and being part of a team. My varsity football team was full of top talent, but we never translated that to the games and wound up with two disappointing, four-win seasons. After college, I played semiprofessionally for a championship team, but we were just a bunch of older men trying to relive our glory days. But there was a difference; when it came time to play, there was a level of communication and commitment to the man by your side unlike anything I had experienced before.

In high tech, I have met more than a few technologists with type A, individualistic personalities, and very fixed mindsets. They are self-absorbed and arrogant, and only interested in what they want to achieve to the dismissal of everyone else. Corporations are starting to learn from sports and have found that companies that focus on the team vs. the individual are five times more likely to be high performing. Having a growth mindset and a team mentality has given me a much broader, wider impact. And it just feels better getting to the finish line, looking to your left and right, and your teammates are there beside you.

7. Complete vs. Compete – I am not going to go as deep as I could on this one, but this is a particular pet peeve of mine. As a Black man, I am often challenged by the next man up. There are unconscious biases by leaders who allow it and by those who introduce it. A new person joins the team, and in the context of "learning or being curious," she starts building connections and plans with portions of the project that I am leading. We should all know our roles and really lock in on delivering on them. That is what we hire people to do. When a teammate starts working on someone else's assignments, it turns into a competition. This behavior is seditious and undermining. What is interesting is that typically we only see this level of comfort-crossing boundaries when certain minorities or a woman is in leadership. Sorry; I know I need to make this positive.

Let me put it this way: we all have skills, we're all smart and ambitious. The best way to win championships is to be a great team player. Never take out a teammate's legs. It's a sign of low integrity and disrespect. And it hurts.

8. Quality over Quantity – A lot of us are trying to deliver too many things at once and, as a result, the impact is not as great. Sometimes you may have to drop a ball or two. What I have learned is that corporations don't really see the seven balls in the air. They see the three that are on the floor. I

subscribe to the rule of three. I would rather deliver three things really well than seven things poorly.

Raise your hand if you would fly in an airplane if you knew there was a 30% chance it's going to crash. Bring that mindset to delivering quality work reliably and you will expand your impact.

9. Change! See the bigger picture! – I have dedicated an entire chapter to change. The premise here is that as technologists, we have to adapt to change in a much more accelerated pace than any profession that I know. We have to be committed to being lifelong learners to keep pace. To break past traditional, educational, and even racial barriers, we must meet change head on. Charles Darwin captures this sentiment profoundly when he stated, "It's not the strongest or smartest of a species that survives, but the ones that adapt." The bible says it this way: "The race is not given to the swift or the strong, but to the one who endures to the end."

10. Show Value! – As professionals, it is important for us to be able to tell our story. How did we impact the bottom line? What did we do to drive value? If you are unable to clearly communicate your victories, you are really missing the point of it all. This is fundamental for growth in technology.

11. Better over Bitter – Life is going to throw you curve balls. There will be setbacks, disappointments, and failures, but don't let these sever your spirit. Once you've gone through a trying time, sit back and reassess yourself. Have you become callous and hardened because of the trauma? Have you lost your passion? Are you now operating in auto drive, performing from muscle memory? I talk about this in detail in the chapter on change, but I'll say this right here-you have to retake your joy! I had to do this through counselling at a very low point in my life. Once I found my joy and chose to become better over bitter, it opened the doors for an accomplishment that I never dreamed I would have.

Chapter 9:
THE LITTLE DAD THAT COULD (WHAT ARE THE ODDS!)

The little dad that could, surrounded by my beautiful wife and children

I always had the highest regard for my family, and I knew that someday I would have a large family of my own. When I was sixteen and saw my wife for the first time, the first thought that popped in my head was, "Wow, that is the marrying kind!" Of course, my mind translated this to mean "*she is* so *out of your league. She's well above average. You would be fortunate if she speaks back.*"

When I thought about being a father, it was important to me to provide for my family what I did not have: a father, present and involved. Yolanda and I doted on our children and did our best to raise them well. We had a great support system with family close by. My children grew up knowing their great grandparents, grandparents, aunties, uncles, and cousins. We also had an excellent church community, Fellowship of Faith Church, International, where we were involved and plugged in. Three of my children attended Southwest Atlanta Christian Academy (SACA), and the others, after pre-k, had to initially go to public school.

I relocated to Redmond Washington for Microsoft in 2003 and relocated back to Atlanta in 2006. When my family relocated back, Sister Gerri Thompson made sure that all my children were able to attend SACA, so all of my children were able to eventually attend private school. I am sure that I paid some, but basically, she provided scholarships to my kids. For that I am eternally grateful.

Raising our crew was an amazing journey. We were not rich, and we were far from perfect, but there was plenty of love to go around. I tried to instill a since of identity in my family, to make sure that Jarah, Abigail, Dwight Jr., Amelia, Dean and David knew exactly what it meant to be a *Jones*. We spent a lot of family time together. We laughed, loved, and supported each other. We stuffed our bellies at buffets like Ryans or Old Country Buffet, enjoyed family movie nights watching the latest Veggie Tales or Disney movies, and took great pleasure in family vacations at our time share in Hilton Head Island, S.C.

We had high expectations for how we dressed and our behavior at home and in public. My wife and I did our best to instill morals and Christian values into our children. We actively participated in their education and knew their teachers. We tried our best to model the highest values before our offspring.

For the most part, I think we did a good job. Please note that my definition of Christian "is a sinner saved by grace." I am a Christian man who happens to be Black, or at least that's my aspiration.

Oftentimes I get out of order and become a Black man that happens to be Christian. I am sure a lot of that will come out in this book, but my goal is for my children to see that I place Jesus over everything. Where I fall short, have been weak or even failed, He has made me strong and whole, and He will do the same for them.

Being a Black man means the journey has not been kind. There is a societal pecking order, and you are often placed on the bottom. Our biggest detractors can be our fellow Americans, the media, our community and even ourselves. We look at each other with a very critical eye, quick to find fault, and we'll fight each other before we will fight with someone who does not look like us. We do not trust the man in the mirror, so our women and children have a very tough time seeing us as leaders, especially since so many of my Brothers are absent from the home. The ones who are in the home are constantly overloaded with pressures from a society that views them as second class. And sadly, your value can be easily undermined, even in your own home!

Unfortunately, we live in a world that promotes escape routes and traps, planted in everything from our music to traffic stops that threaten our safety and too often, our lives. My approach to being a father, husband and leader has really changed over time. The lens that others see me through can be clouded by a malicious programming that says anything or anyone is better than you. This means that a lot of the decisions and victories happen DESPITE how I am seen, and can only be appreciated after the results are in.

I have learned to be okay with this because this distorted lens strengthens my relationship with God. The things I have learned make Fatherhood, Leader, and Manhood no longer just titles, but who I am. I *live* these roles because I *am* these roles. I am not trying to bail or be brave. I am just trying to live up to the call on my life the best I can.

As a father, I have always tried to be available to my children. I am by no means perfect in this, but I have tried. Having six children, I knew there was no way I could always be there for each one of them, but I tried to support each of their personal ambitions. Most of my children played sports, so in that arena I was able to give lots of support. Showing that I was there for practice and for the game was my way of demonstrating that I was there for them, and that they were extremely important to me.

Sports was my vehicle, but I did have one child who did not give a flying flip about being an athlete. So, instead of supporting Amelia from the bleachers, I brought her to live with me during my time away from the family.

My attempts were not perfect. I failed a lot. One of my disappointments was not being able to afford the tuition to support my child Abigail through college. She did graduate and is successful today, but knowing she had to change paths because I was not able to support her dream is a tough pill to swallow.

One of the scariest things about being a Black man and specifically, a Black man in tech, is that when my work is done, there might not be a historical record of me being there and the impact that I made. I have a buddy who served with me on several Blacks at Microsoft committees and made a difference in our community. One day he was suddenly let go, and that was it! His technical legacy was done.

As a father, husband and professional, legacy is very important to me. Just as important as it is for me to lay a foundation with the work I am doing, it's equally as critical for me to bring others along. Starting with my family. I have read in the bible that your ministry starts at home. How can I share my message of success for the masses, but not be able to bring my own family along? This is a bit harder than it looks. I don't think that anyone in my family, other than me, had a career in tech as their first choice. I actually believe it was the opposite. My wife and children set out on their own paths, and a couple of my children have not chosen tech, and I am totally okay with that. But somewhere along the way, a few of my children got the vision that they could have well-paying and lasting careers in technology, and they never looked back.

So how did this happen? Each one of them has their own story about how they made their way to technical careers, but I think it all started with the exposure to Microsoft when we first moved to Redmond from Atlanta. In my years in technology positions in Atlanta, my wife and children had very limited access to what I did at the office. When I joined Microsoft, this all changed.

We ascended to a quality of life that we had never been exposed to, stemming, in part, from how the entire city of Redmond revolves around Microsoft. Our medical insurance was fully paid with no co-pay, we had access to the professional sports club that was one of the best in America, we lived in a city where there were years between murders, and there was freedom to create and be yourself without constraint. Gone was the need to act like, or dress like, sister or brother so and so. No longer were we confined by our limiting views of never wanting to leave Atlanta. We were allowed to see and experience life outside our sphere, and it was just as okay for us to be in these new spaces as anyone else.

Microsoft was totally family-friendly, and my family often joined me at work. Dwight, Amelia, Dean and David would walk to my job after school through trails that connected the community to the campus. My entire family was able to attend awesome Microsoft events like the annual company picnic held on a massive farm on the side of a mountain. What a glorious time! My family had full access to all the food they wanted; there was rock climbing, pony rides and bumper cars, and concerts exclusively for Microsoft employees and their families.

My children were allowed to go trick or treating from building to building on Halloween, collecting as much candy as they could haul. And of course, every time they came around, all the drinks were free. Some buildings had *Xbox* and other gaming systems or pool tables and ping pong, all free and accessible to them. They also volunteered with me on the *Day of Caring* and were with me during *Bring Your Child to Work* events. All of this planted seeds that took all of us to a very different level of exposure, privilege, and access, one where we were active and welcome participants.

Things really kicked into high gear in 2005 when I brought Jarah's entire graduating class from Atlanta to the Microsoft-sponsored *Digigirlz* Technology camp. The young ladies were taught coding and many other important skills by professional women. A key moment for Jarah was when a female executive, who led the 30-billion-dollar Microsoft Office business, asked for someone to stand up and introduce themselves. Jarah, who was normally reserved, broke out of her cocoon that day. She raised her hand, stood up and spread her wings for the first time. She proudly introduced herself to a room of over 100 people. The speaker gave her $20 for having the courage to go first and push past her fears. She went on to use that example to teach the room a lesson. This was the moment I had been waiting for for Jarah!

The courageous moment when Jarah Jones' (18), hand raised high (left) introduced herself first (right) at Digigirlz in 2005

More of the young ladies that I sponsored at Digigirlz in 2005

Those young ladies saw many women in leadership who encouraged and exposed them to careers in technology. My boys, who didn't participate in the camp, helped me facilitate the events. These early experiences gave my children the vision and aspiration to go for the gold in technical roles.

I also believe the friendliness of my coworkers and managers, who were also my friends, made a big difference, especially in my early Microsoft days. People like my managers Ken Patchett, Monika Machado, and Ray Austria, who were really like extended family members and really came through for us.

My senior manager, Ken, once invited my entire family to his home for 4th of July. Fireworks were illegal in Georgia, but not in Washington. He gave my seven and eight-year-old sons firecrackers and they recreated Independence Day with Ken's entire community. My family's mind was blown by the acceptance and love of coworkers outside of work.

The same for Monika and Ray. Both were my managers, but we were also close friends, having fun and watching our families grow up together. I could borrow Ken's truck, and I rented a house from Ray. All this is normally taboo, but this team loved my family and wanted to support our success. Working with them was the best introduction to Microsoft that I could possibly have had. I wish all teams were as close as this one.

Let me be fully transparent here: no nepotism opened the door for my family. They applied, fought for, and landed their positions, starting with my first-born daughter Jarah. After working for a friend's software development company in Atlanta, my 5 foot 4, former point guard, promoted-to-wife-and -mother, caramel-skinned beauty of a daughter took the initiative, applied, and earned her full-time job. She didn't tell me till after the fact. I didn't even get a referral bonus!

My wife followed suit and landed a similar role as Jarah. (I guess Jarah got her referral bonus).

My next child, my 4-foot 11-inch giant, was destined to be a doctor, but after fighting to get into medical school, she took an admin role for a small tech company in Bellevue, WA. The managers saw her potential, and she was promoted four times in about five years (sounds familiar). She rapidly outgrew that company and, after a few coaching sessions with her dad, she applied at Microsoft and scored a full-time opportunity.

My two sons' paths were totally different. Dean earned an internship as part of *Year-Up*, an accelerated, no-nonsense college vocational program that teaches underrepresented kids technical and business skills. You have to be 100% committed to graduate and get an internship. Dean graduated and interned as a program manager for a Microsoft Digital team for a year. Then he went back to his studies and completed his undergraduate degree.

David earned his undergraduate degree from Washington State University in two years then began applying for Microsoft jobs. Neither one of them was having much success applying for jobs, but then a program came up where I was able to refer them both and they hit paydirt!

I am humbled and extremely proud to have my children following my footsteps as technology professionals. It feels good to know that the field I work in is robust enough to provide them with careers that they can continue to build on, if they choose to.

Chapter 10:
GRATITUDE!

You know, it would be easy for me to point to this book and say "Hey, if you follow my ten easy steps, I guarantee your success." Of course, it's not that simple but I think it's smart to take the lessons I have learned to help improve your experience and avoid some of my mistakes.

But I also know that technology is a buffet of opportunity, and you just need to find your salad bar. You need to come in hungry, and humble, with an appetite to learn and grow. You also need to know you cannot get there alone. Your degree, your charisma and your brain are not enough. You will need help along the way.

Let's start with God. I am at the point in my life where I know that God + me is a majority. My Heavenly Father runs it all. He is the Father of the universe and if He be for me, who can be against me? He has made a way out of no way so many times. I haven't done the math, but getting to my level of success, in my mind is on par with being a number 1 NFL or NBA pic. Another shout out to the Howard family.

My own personal walk has been about adapting to constant change. There has been a lot of breaking down and rebuilding along the way, and I know for a fact I wouldn't be here if it were not for certain people helping me succeed. I am not talking about mentors, sponsors, or coaches. I am talking about my hidden network, those angels disguised as men and women.

I've had a few of these guiding lights carry me and my family during the darkest times. They were there for me during my worst nightmare when I could not provide for my family. I'll never forget how desperately I tried to save myself when my technical career was disrupted by a market shift, layoff, or the end of my usefulness.

I'm telling you this to warn you that your level of commitment to the technical industry will be challenged. You will have many opportunities to walk away. My road was not always easy. There were bumps, potholes, and detours, but today I can say it was worth it.

But listen, I don't want you to focus on my trials. I want you to see how God put people in my life who had such a heart for me that they were willing to help carry me during my tribulations.

God has a purpose for my life and for yours. He ordered my steps and sent people to pick me up at my lowest points. I think of Haggar and her son Ishmael in the desert, when she thought they would die of thirst, but God made a provision. The angel told her that her son would become a great nation before they took the first sip of lifesaving water. I had angels too. They saw my value even when I did not. They nurtured me and got me to a point where I could get back up and fight again.

You, dear reader, set yourself up for success each time you get up when you've been knocked to the ground. Here are some of my angels:

Pastor Wayne C. Thompson who counseled me, encouraged me, and reminded me that what God did with my first job, He was able to do again.

Mr. Keith Cheney and Ms. Shan Cheney provided a job that transitioned me into consulting after I lost my position at WH Smith. They allowed me to work as a Sr. Systems Architect for Bank of America and gave me my first experience on the Windows Server environment. He provided income for me when I was on the bench and not bringing in any money. I am forever grateful for this.

My dear brother, Srinath Duddilla, who brought me in as an account manager in his firm SunPlus Data Group, Inc., and allowed me to learn the consulting world under his mentorship. This gentleman of the highest degree paid me as I learned, and eventually allowed me to consult through his firm for Norfolk Southern Railway and BellSouth Internet Services as I gained Microsoft and Cisco Certifications.

One of my best friends (and frat brother) Robert Nicholas Dumas and his wife Kenya Palmer Dumas. They found me down and out after the dot-bomb era had decimated technical jobs and destructive accounting practices had destroyed the consulting industry in the early 2000s. He hired me to work at his day care business where I got to reconnect with him, Kenya, and their parents for many priceless moments. I am forever grateful for these sabbaticals in my technical journey. They forced me to retool and refresh, and the relationships, bonding and lessons learned made the time-out so nourishing and great preparation for what came next.

I finally want to truly thank ALL those I've worked with over the years. Each one of you is part of my story, and I am thankful for your contributions to my success. I am ashamed that there are so many names I've left out, but here are a few.

Financial Services Corporation: My late sister Deborah Mary Jones Weaver who helped me land the meeting with Brad Thompson, the VP of Management Information Systems, whom I met for a college project that led to my first job.

Esther Hill, Lula Walker, Brent Guyton, Chris Heffner, Helen Prater, Robin Mauldin, Bill Billera, Roger Greenwood.

Decatur Federal Savings and Loan: Daniel Wade, Wally Woodard, Bob Lahl, Randy Heller, Thomas Maddox, Donald Gates.

WH Smith: CEO John Hancock, CIO Kevin Phillips, Raleigh Waltower, Thomas Maddox, Mike Mann, Sunny Duddilla, Donald Gates.

Creative Source Unlimited: Keith Cheney, Shan Cheney, and James Harris.

SunPlus Data Group: Sunny and Sri Deepa Duddilla, Ravi Mekala, Sri Duddilla, Vani Duddilla, Vijaya Sree, Satya Baskar, and so many others.

Norfolk Southern Railway: Dexter Grindstaff, who allowed me to meet with him before 5 am TWICE to land this job.

Alvin Ross, Carissa Thompson, Chuck Foy, the honorable USMC Ret. Master Gunnery Seargent Clyde Buster Herrin, Aquilles Campos, Gabriel Vannice and a host of others in the NOC and Support Desk.

BellSouth Internet Services: Mark Thompson, Sally Scarborough, Brian Lynn, Donna Burr, Lisa Bullock, Andrew Julye, Wender Bulloch, Helen Allen, Chris Parks.

Then there is my Microsoft family, co-workers, managers, and vendors. I am so grateful for each and every one of you. It took the entire village to bring me this far down the road. I can't wait to meet those angels who will walk with me the rest of the way.

The final Dwightism that I am sharing, hot off the press by the way, comes from the time I spent brainstorming how I wanted to write this chapter. Literally, I started by writing a list of names of people who have been with me on my tech quest and have enriched me in some way or another.

My cup runneth over with gratitude for the many friends and colleagues who've been there for me along the way. We are only separated by distance.

You see, no matter what I share with you or how I tell you my story, it looks easy because it's all told from the rearview mirror.

What you cannot see is the height of each mountain, the width of my canyons, how deep the oceans were for the Mr. Nobody I believed I was.

This is what I think I have most in common with my father, and his father, and my culture and with you.

The final Dwightism is Desperation Over Privilege. Understanding this changes your approach to everything. As I'm being coached to write this book, I've been desperate to get my story committed to pen and paper, to share these words, and to highlight African American's great contributions to technology. I had this book burning inside of me like a struck match.

I've been trying to tell this story during Black history month or Juneteenth events, but the audience was not big enough to really affect change. So, when I saw an opportunity to receive guidance on writing a book in the final days of Microsoft's annual GIVE charity event, I outbidded everyone. Why? Because I knew it was the vehicle I had been searching for and the perfect way to share my story with a larger audience.

I had been wanting to write this book for more than ten years. There were about ten of us in the class, each of us bursting with stories we thought were compelling. Some of the students were already authors and were there to learn this system for writing and publishing books. By the time we were three classes in, we were all in different phases of our writing journeys.

Our assignment, due on a Friday, was to have the first of twelve chapters written and to have made a schedule to write a chapter every two weeks. Well, this is my ninth chapter, I have hired an editor, and I am committed to having this book published on my dad's birthday. It all comes down to this: I am desperate to get this story out. I want to shine a light in the darkness and say, "Hey, there is a way," to those of you who see yourselves in my story.

I must admit, I am a bit nervous that I don't have what it takes to finish this book, but I am so grateful for this open door that I have been praying for, practicing for, freewriting for for so many years. Lord don't let me blow it! The point is, I see this as more than just a class assignment; it's the open window I have been praying for, and I am not taking this opportunity for granted.

I believe this story is bigger than me. It's part of God's plan for me, so I am approaching it with deep hunger, appreciation, and gratitude. The other students probably don't see it that way. After all, you bid money, you win the class and you're in. You attend the class, learn the process, and if you write a book, fine. If you don't. Fine. There's nothing wrong with this. My classmates have different motivations from mine. My reason is personal, full of desperation, and that's what truly matters to me.

I think of desperation as the skill that has helped me become a Black technologist, and that keeps me relevant today. Desperation was the key when I found an Introduction to Computers course and got my first job. I was failing in college and seriously searching for direction. When I got the opportunity, there was no way I was going to drop the ball.

There were so many times I was down for the count, overwhelmed by the weight of this life, and more than a few people witnessed my despair. Ask them where I was when they provided a helping hand. They have all seen me at rock bottom and have invested their time, money and resources in me and my family. They've given me jobs to help me weather the storm and get back on track. I cannot fail in this opportunity, and I am forever grateful for those people.

I have a question for you: do you have a sense of desperation or a sense of privilege? There's nothing wrong with privilege, and yes you may belong in the room, but what happens if there are setbacks beyond your control, like a downturn in the economy or a once-opened door closes? How would you pry the door open again? How do you get up to face your opponent when he is bigger and faster than you and has been eating your lunch every day? What about when you've been told it doesn't matter what you've accomplished, your education or your experience, the answer is still no?

This is where I cry out to God! I know He hears me. I know He sees me, and I know that He has brought me out of so many storms. Hear me when I say, when no one else can help you, He will. When your education is not enough, when there are layoffs, He will make a way out of no way. I can remember spending hours before the Lord, praying and listening to Fred Hammond's cd "Spirit of David" over and over. The track I couldn't stop playing, *"Song of Strength"* with the lyrics *"Hold on and wait just a little while, He'll bring a song of strength in the midnight, touch our lives with Your loving hand, Hold On, Hold On…"*

I have been in a place where no human could see or help me, but God has always been with me. I don't know who this is for, but if you are lost and desperate, that is a good place to be. Cry out to God and see if He will not make a way out of no way for you!

What happens after you have been desperately praying and waiting for one shot of hope? What happens when the opportunity comes? You know the answer. There is no second guessing. You leap through that window of opportunity because you know that it was opened by God. You are a brand-new creature, breathing the pure air of spirit. The same space that I enter through gratitude and desperation is the same room that others enter through privilege. The living room that is your miracle is the bedroom that some people step into with ease.

Let's deconstruct that for just a moment: I work in a company where there are many, many talented people. Everyone is smart. Many are there because they planned for it, had access to education, put the work in and made it. But there are quite a few who had to overcome long odds of bias and inequality.

Like Rekha. She is from a small village of Peruvemba in Keralain, India where she had to fetch water every day before she went to school. She was born with darker skin and as a result, she was shunned in her community. She was told that she would not be successful because her skin wasn't fair. Nevertheless, Rekha became a proud Microsoft employee.

Even with all the progress I've made, I have not even scratched the surface. I'm at a level 65 but the highest peak you can reach is level 80 or above! There are so many of my people fighting to reach my level of success, not realizing that there is much higher ground to which they can aspire.

Will it be you who makes it to those upper levels? This is my dream for you!

Chapter 11:
INNOVATION AND THE FALSE NARRATIVE

As I start wrapping up this book, I want to make sure you know that a career in technology can change your entire life if you're willing to invest yourself in the profession. Technical genius and innovation do not see race, creed, or national origin; there are so many inventions and advancements that were born in the brilliant hearts and minds of my people. Unfortunately, because they were just outside the spotlight's shine, the genesis of so many inventions have been lost by time, capitalism, and greed.

I shared with you how some of the inventions by Black technologists have been the reason behind the success of many technology companies. I stand in awe and honor of pioneers like Jesse Eugene Russell, inventor of the digital cell phone; Dr. James West inventor of the electret microphone; Dr. Marian Croak developer of Voice over IP (VOIP) technology, and Jerry Lawson inventor, of the first cartridge-based gaming system.

The digital divide continues to widen because of the access that some have to technical jobs and the ability to grow *their* career because *they* are deemed more worthy than Black people. HBCUs and White universities are turning out Black graduates with technical degrees every year, so when corporations claim they can't find talent or groom managers from the African American community, it's a lie built on bias. You cannot convince me that a world-leading, US-based technology company can only attract and retain 4% of their talent and 4% of their managers from a pool of *every* Black person on *every* continent, in *every* country in the world! You are discrediting an entire race to explain your lack of diversity. This is a false narrative and must change. Although I am hopeful for the future as I have seen more commitment and a slight uptick in Black hires, there is still an incredible amount of work to be done.

There is so much opportunity in technology. My challenge to you is to pick a tech company or a job site and just perform a random search. In my own company, I receive at least one email a day, sometimes four or more, announcing that some group has opened a new job. There is big demand for technical talent. Your challenge will be finding an area that appeals to you and gaining fundamental knowledge through education, training and/or certifications. You will then need to fight for the opening that will get you your first opportunity. Remember (SAT)H Success = Attitude + Technical Ability times Hours applied.

Once you score your first role, you must remain relevant. Technology is constantly changing so you must have the mindset of a lifelong learner. Expect that you will need to reinvent yourself every two to four years to remain relevant. Also expect that there will be some changes that you cannot anticipate like layoffs, market shifts, etc. Develop the skill of desperation. There is no entitlement in technology. You have to be willing to not give up despite the no's, in order to stay in the field. It will not be easy; there will be cuts and bruises along the way, but it will be worth it.

There is no salary ceiling and there is no shortage of jobs. You are only limited by your ambition and your ability to be shaped and transformed into the level of technical excellence that you want to achieve. But you are going to have to be willing to change. Where you are today, and what may have helped you climb to your present level, is only the start. You must adapt and grow to see the bigger picture.

I have changed and transformed a great deal in my tenure. The way I thought about processes and procedures had to evolve or I would not have survived. I've had to allow my mind to be torn down and rebuilt to keep pace.

I used to think about things in a waterfall way; one thing taking place after the other, constructed with exacting standards until you finally deliver a product. This may be okay for the transportation industry where you must build a perfect airplane or make sure trains do not collide, but for the technical industry it is about speed to market. I had to learn agile methods which are all about getting the product to market fast and iterating quickly based on feedback.

What does this all mean? You must find the right company and/or the right opportunity, be willing to change and grow within the company (or outside of it) in order to do well in tech and have a career at least as good as mine.

After thirty-six years, I consider my career middle of the road. Remember at Microsoft there are more than fifteen levels higher than mine. I may not come close to reaching the uppermost levels, but my hope is that I will light a flame inside YOU that will compel YOU to reach much higher heights than I have.

Remember, no one gets there alone. You will need help along the way, but some of that support needs to come from those corporations that have allowed the digital divide to persist. They need to do the right thing and investigate the data as it relates to the treatment of Blacks in pursuit of technical careers. There also needs to be a pipeline supported by a welcoming environment embracing and encouraging the next generation of technologists. We need to holler from the rooftops about the contributions of Black technologists so that future generations will know they too can be a blessed source of innovation to our country and the world.

Chapter 12:
HELP NEEDED

More than ever, we are in a time where we must consider each other and the greater good. People are hurting and even dying from a global pandemic and its downstream impacts. Our society is eroding from political divisiveness and the inaction that literally has allowed people to die unnecessarily and has threatened even the fabric of America's democracy. We have always known that we should love our brothers and sisters, but I have not seen, in my lifetime, where it has been this front and center. Where decisions like, will I wear a mask or take a vaccine so that I do not bring a deadly disease to my fellowman or woman, or do I approve of an overzealous weaponized neighbor or empowered police officer for taking the life of unarmed citizens, or do I side with a tyrannical leader who could care less, even for his own constituents? Dr. King said it this way, "The time is always right to do what is right."

I am hurting from a personal loss. On Christmas eve 2021, my great nephew Benny walked into a Walmart to steal a couple of dolls, a ball, and a box of cereal so that his girlfriend's daughter would have gifts for Christmas. However, he got caught, and he had a weapon and was shot and killed by authorities.

As I play this out over and over in my mind, I cannot come to a rational reason for him to do this. We know that he was working two minimum wage jobs and had to use public transportation to make ends meet, but he has family that loves him and is from a law enforcement family. He could have asked any of us for a hundred dollars. Although the only contact that we have had for years is over Facebook. Benny's journey brought him to a point of desperation to provide for his family, when so many of us can walk through a Walmart with privilege and spend a hundred bucks. His desperation drove him to a poor choice that cost him his life.

Benny couldn't see his way out of lack. He is one very painful example of those who do not know what tomorrow will bring, their backs are against the wall, and they see no way to bridge the social economic divide. My prayer is that our government, technical corporations, and local leaders will see the tremendous opportunity that technology provides to uplift people and change their paradigm. Benny only made it to 30 before his life was snuffed out, and per my high school counsellor, that was where I should have been too. But by God's grace and mercy, through my journey in technology my life was changed. There is so much opportunity in technology. It is an infinitely sweet pie, and there is enough for us all to have our own slice.

Know this; I have made it to an admirable place in my tech journey. I no longer live in lack. I have crossed the threshold to prosperity. I have built a legacy to sustain my children that allows them not just to live, but to thrive. It was not a given path; it took a lot of prayer, perseverance, and assistance to make my dream come true. Let my words be the wake-up call to say, I don't care who you are or where you came from, someone helped you along the way.

My first helper was my unsung hero, my mother. She laid it all down for her children and gave everything she had to keep the family moving. She is a fiery, light-skinned, curly haired dynamo with a bible always in her hand or in her car. She ministered to the homeless and fed the poor. She can't get around like she used to, but her mind is still as sharp as when she was a little girl. She worked double shifts from 3-11pm, then 11pm – 7am to make ends meet for $7.50 an hour, but where her physical strength ended, her faith was strong. My father was gone, but we weren't on welfare. We were on faithfare!

I did not have to leave home to find Jesus. I learned about Him from Mama. She cried out to Him, counted on Him, and I've watched Him carry her to live a life of over ninety-six years. She raised many generations of her family, and she does not want a reward. Not from me or you. The only real way you can bless her is by demonstrating that you are also walking with the Lord.

Transitioning from my mother to my favorite American hero, I want to uplift the life of Harriett Tubman. Listen up all my marathon buddies: for Harriet Tubman to escape slavery, she had to walk 100 miles alone in the woods, mostly at night, without provision. Can we pause, close our eyes for a moment and let that sink in? There was not any route planning, mile markers, food, or water stations. Only, a life-or-death situation and a sense of desperation could drive her to undertake such treacherous journeys, but she had already determined that the risk of death was not going to deter her. She said, "There was one of two things I had a right to: liberty or death. If I could not have one, I would take the other, for no man should take me alive. I should fight for liberty as long as my strength lasted." She first tried to escape with her brothers, but they were not ready to change and see the bigger picture, so after that failed, she escaped on her second try, alone.

There are parts of her story that are underplayed but I understand why. What she accomplished and her will, faith and perseverance are the showpiece, but Ms. Tubman could not have escaped without a place to escape to. I am grateful for the abolitionists, the Quakers, and the lawmakers who outlawed slavery and provided her a safe haven called "The Underground Railroad."

None of us can get where we're going alone. We all need help. Mother Harriet needed help, and so will you if your quest is to take ground and break ground in technology.

But wait a minute, I get it. We are asking a forward-looking industry to think like the abolitionists, to follow the teachings of Jesus and leave the 99 that are doing great to find the one. I am a father of six, and to be honest, I raised them in a way that is similar to the way corporations think. Frankly I have children that I need to come back for, meaning I raised them into adulthood, but they may need a bit more support to reach their goals, and I have not completed that work. I need to do some Harriet-ing myself!

This is sort of what we are asking corporations to do; acknowledge that the company is doing great but look back and help those who are being left behind. It's a tall order for me as a father, and I can only imagine the challenge to the leadership. But isn't that what the compassionate states and the decent people did for Harriet?

The point is we would not know about this courageous, powerful woman if it were not for the commitment of several forces all pulling together to secure the freedom of a people so hideously oppressed.

Ms. Tubman could have escaped then gotten married and lived out her days as a free person. I am sure there were other escaped slaves who did just that. But she felt compelled to continue to work for the liberation of her people and understood that it was not enough to secure her own freedom. This "Woman called Moses" knew she had a purpose far bigger than herself. She completed thirteen missions, risking it all to free enslaved people. She was hunted as an outlaw, but she never lost a single soul on the bloody, tear-soaked trail. Once she led the 100-mile journey with thirteen souls in about five days. She personally freed about seventy slaves and provided instructions to free many more, without an ounce of training. What do my marathoners and Mt. Everest hikers think of that?

Tubman's story does not end there. She was a wife, mother, and patriot. She led a band of scouts under the orders of the US Secretary of War, Edwin Stanton. She was also the first woman to lead and advise the Union Army on an armed assault during the Civil War. When soldiers destroyed plantations and rescued more than 750 slaves, the newspapers noted Mrs. Tubman's "patriotism, sagacity, energy and ability." What an American Hero!

I love her story. It reminds me that I am on the right track as I try to do the right thing and reach back to my community. It's not enough for me, my four and no more. I've gotta reach out and reach back until my shoulders are sore and my arthritis tells me to go somewhere and sit down.

I sincerely hope that technology companies will see the disparity and the disadvantages, lean in, and offer help. Harriet couldn't do it alone, and our world is better because of the alliances that made her work possible. I wonder what type of America we would live in if the South had won the civil war. What would our place be in the world's economy?

There is so much work to be done by corporations, employee readiness groups, allies, and sponsors to help close the divide. Of course, we'll continue creating and innovating but we need the opportunity to do this in proportion to the size and scale of our community, while providing hope for the college graduates and technical experts of the future. You need to know that just as technology has provided a career path for so many, it can provide for you, too. The only ceiling is the one in your bedroom.

The good news is help appears to be on the way. As I mentioned earlier, this year I saw real forward movement for our community in *Microsoft's Diversity and Inclusion Report*. They announced the most positive results I've ever seen. In addition, Microsoft Senior leadership shared specific goals to double the number of Blacks and Hispanics in management and executive roles. I know that Microsoft is committed, and I am optimistic that great things for Black people are on the horizon. NOW IS THE TIME, IF YOU ARE BLACK AND INTERESTED IN TECHNOLOGY, TO LEAN IN AND DOUBLE DOWN YOUR EFFORTS. Change is coming. Tomorrow holds promise and a bright, beautiful future for us. For you.

Here's my speech from Black History Month 2021, "I Am in The Room"

I am in the room.

> Martin Luther King once said, "it's all right to tell a man to lift himself by his own bootstraps, but it is cruel jest to say to a bootless man that he ought to lift himself by his own bootstraps."

> Out of the night that covers me, Black as the pit from pole to pole, I thank whatever gods may be For my unconquerable soul. "Invictus" (Ernest Henly)

> Dr. King went on to say, "It's even worse to tell a man to lift himself by his own bootstraps when somebody is standing on the boot."

I am in the room.

> If you can keep your head when all about you Are losing theirs and blaming it on you,

> If you can trust yourself when all men doubt you, But make allowance for their doubting too;

> If you can wait and not be tired by waiting, Or being lied about, don't deal in lies,

> Or being hated, don't give way to hating, And yet don't look too good, nor talk too wise:

> ...If you can fill the unforgiving minute With sixty seconds' worth of distance run,

> Yours is the Earth and everything that's in it, And - which is more - you'll be a Man, my son!

> If (Rudyard Kipling)

I am in the room.

As I reflect on Black History Month and what message I can deposit this year, I want to continue to encourage those that are joined with me in the struggle. I want to educate those who are new to the message or who are considering it from afar. Finally, I extend the perpetual olive branch of peace to people on the fringe who are questioning, "Why are we even talking about Black History at all?"

I think about the past messages I have shared. From the origins of Black History Month to the contribution to technology through invention and ideation by Black technologists, to shedding light on the huge digital divide that has left people like me behind through systematic oppression, red lining, and workplace bias. To the unsung heroes of this country like my favorite Harriett Tubman, whose innate gifts were emboldened by the Black and White allies and sponsors that shared her conviction to cause.

My message today is one of self-reflection for the purpose of shared hope. Why? Because 2020 was one big dumpster fire that is still burning and impacting us all. However, we are united in purpose. We are all doing our part to fight hidden enemies and to overcome this pandemic in order to put our world back on track. A world where words like truth, honor, faith, integrity, and justice do not have to be second guessed.

Well, what does any of this have to do with Black history month? I was born and raised in Atlanta, Georgia, the birthplace of many civil rights leaders. Home to such leaders as Martin Luther King, Benjamin E. Mays, Julian Bond, Andrew Young, and John Lewis, just to name a few. A place where Black people have bled and died in a fight to get this nation to lead with their hearts and not their heads. Where people in the ruling class have used legislation and hidden agendas to subvert conscious and suppress people of color.

Well, I watched my state of Georgia and my family and friends (who are the sons and daughters of the civil rights era), stand again as the conscience of America. They voted in 2020 and helped this country take a stand and say no to an oppressive administration, that lied to us on the very existence of a pandemic, denied science at the cost in the hundreds of thousands of lives, uplifted a white supremacist mindset, put children in cages and separated them from their parents. This threatened the very core of our democracy. With more than 74 million voters in tow, being okay with some or all of the above. So, let the record be clear that it was the Black people in this country that made the difference and swayed the pendulum towards hope, equality, and justice.

It does not matter where you are from, I know that we can all identify with the struggles of the past couple of years. How it is front and center in all of our lives. From the killings of George Floyd, Breanna Taylor, Ahmaud Arbery, to the daily death counts of Covid, we are all in this together. It makes the words "we shall overcome" even more meaningful. And guess what many of us are overcoming? Pain, grief, the impact and noise of closed doors and livelihood disruptions. We are still overcoming. We are here today, and we are all in the room.

As the poet Maya Angelou shared,

"Bringing the gifts that my ancestors gave,

I am the dream and hope of the slave.

I rise, I rise, I rise."

And yes! I am in the room!

Chapter 13:
MORE WORK TO BE DONE!

"We must rapidly begin the shift from a "thing-oriented" society to a "person-oriented" society. When machines and computers, profit motives and property rights are considered more important than people, the giant triplets of racism, materialism, and militarism are incapable of being conquered."

Martin Luther King, Jr.

sofreshandsogreen.com

When addressing my former Core Service Engineering and Operations (CSEO) leadership team in 2018, I told them, "I am on a mission to fill cities such as Redmond, Bellevue, Kirkland (all wealthy cities that are in Martin Luther King County in Washington, all with a very low Black population) full of African American and Black families working for Microsoft." You see, I live in Bellevue, and I've lived in Redmond, and for most of my time in those communities, I have had no Black neighbors. There is no Black church, barbershops, soul food restaurants or any of the comforts of the established African American community. I have raised my family in places where they only see *other* races and nationalities in leadership roles.

My family is fortunate. We are from Atlanta, and we know that where we live now is not a true representation of America. Technical companies in this region are going to need to double down to help the Black community get established here. Because of redlining, Seattle made a concerted effort to keep the Black community on the outskirts of prosperity. The social and economic divide was intentionally engineered and executed. Only rarely have families like my own been able to capitalize on the opportunities provided here.

I can bring vision, drive and will to my position all day long, but the US Government, technology corporations and even local leaders, mayors, and council people, must push really hard to affect deep, sustainable change. I challenge them to study the disparities and dig deep to understand the obstacles that plague the African American community, not just put butts in seats. African Americans are challenged to organize but this is no easy assignment, and this country is indifferent about the success of the Black community.

African American workers competing with other countries dedicated to the success of their Black citizens, add another layer of complexity to the mix. I think it is great for our government to sponsor student and work visas and support people from other countries on their technical journey, but they should not receive MORE support or better educational opportunities than your own citizens. Our government should incentivize companies that hire from the African American community and regulate the ones that are only playing lip service to the problems. Corporations need to understand nationalism and that these well-organized countries will have a competitive advantage over African Americans vying for the same jobs. We need a data-driven, holistic approach to solving inequities for the entire African American and Black community.

I have been able to help several Black technologists get hired in my company; however, those victories are few and far between. I shared with you how five members of my family are Microsoft full-time employees, but it took a lot of energy and pushing past no's for them to finally get hired. In other cases, I had to stretch the limits of my ability to reach out to hiring managers on behalf of qualified candidates. Even though I'm in BAM leadership, and in some cases I have leadership support, I would consider my success rate to be only five percent or less. In other words, for every 100 people I have referred, maybe five of them landed jobs. This is a travesty. As a 20-year Microsoft employee, trained to screen candidates, it still takes a miracle to get a candidate from my community through the door. The fulcrum is tilted to screen out verses screen in. How do we change this so that we can bring in Black people in a balanced way, alongside other cultures?

Corporations must acknowledge the problem and be willing to take the challenges head on. I mentioned the success that women are having at Microsoft. I don't think this is by chance. The level of organization and support for women in technology is amazing, as it should be.

Earlier in the book, I talked about how I was able to bring a class of high school girls from Atlanta to the *Digigirlz* camp that Microsoft holds annually. What is amazing is that 30% of the young ladies I sponsored became Microsoft employees, largely due to the exposure they received.

In addition, two of the young men who helped me facilitate the camp also became Microsoft employees. It was, however, unfortunate that although I had donated technology to the school to help build their media center, I was unable to bring any of the Black male students. There is not a Microsoft program to support underrepresented young men of color. I know this was a slap in the face to those talented young men. I was asked directly, "why aren't we going Mr. Jones?" Not having an answer and seeing the pain spread across their faces, also hurt me very deeply. What message did we send by only providing a camp for young ladies?

This leads me to the first investment that needs to be made. Just like Microsoft is invested in *Digigirlz*, we need to make the same type of investment in young boys and men of color. We must understand that the privilege White or Asian men experience in America (and in technology) does not correspond to the experience of the African American male. In fact, it is the opposite. There are programs for young ladies of African American descent, but often their male counterparts find themselves totally left out, far away from the vast land of opportunity.

In 2018, I pushed hard for a pipeline program for young men of color. I am still recovering from the level of pushback I received.

It's crucial that we create relationships to follow African American youth through high school and college and leverage this work to help them obtain their first jobs in technology. I have successfully lived this model, but it has been a lifetime in the making. I need help from willing corporations to take this on, *at scale*, weighing for disadvantage, and making sure that innovative thought, from a shamefully under tapped resource, is valued and maximized.

The next action item is for schools, communities of color and corporations to celebrate Black innovators. If the next generation of Black technologists cannot see themselves in leadership roles, they'll have a hard time aspiring to those same levels of leadership.

I have shown that throughout history, contributions by Black people have been fundamental to the successes of corporations. Even with the high impact they are having, the numbers of Black people working for top technology companies are so low that it's hard to see that Black folks have contributed to the success of these companies. I would love to witness my beloved Atlanta, and my company, make a concerted effort to document and share the contributions of Black people to keep our legacy alive. There should be a National Black Technology Museum and a Black Technology Hall of Fame to celebrate past and present contributions. Curating our accomplishments will allow young technologists to see that there have always been highly intelligent contributors who look just like them.

In my company, there were many Black champions who reached high levels in leadership, but through attrition, or as they retired, their roles were not replaced by other persons of color, so we would lose highly valued pillars of the community. Think about it. All the mentorship, programs, and gains from that single person, lost forever.

This has had a profound effect on the Black employees who remain on staff (who may be three or more levels down from the leader who left the organization). I actually remember closing my office in tears when I would learn we were losing another Black leader. What does this say about the corporate climate? This is a cancer that must be excised, or the tumor of attrition will continue to grow unchecked.

I was recently on a call where we had a guest from the IT Senior Management Forum. This gentleman was the CIO of a large transportation company. He shared with us how, in his career advancement, corporate leaders would seek him out to take on certain roles. Isn't this interesting? In my own case, although I have been a top performer, no corporate leaders would come knocking on my door! My career advancement has been a result of applying and competing. It would be great if, in the high-tech industry, folks were busy seeking out top performers of color and looking to place them in key management and technical roles.

In summary, I believe that it will take a committed effort from federal and local governments, corporations, and community leaders to become super-intentional about closing the digital divide. Our government needs to hold technology companies accountable for their despairingly low number of African American and Black hires and low retention rates. Local governments in cities where there are high numbers of Blacks, need to invest in educational programs, libraries and museums that showcase the amazing contributions to technology by Black people.

We need a Hall of Fame, inside and outside of corporations, so that the legacy left by Blacks that contributed to your bottom line will not be forgotten. Corporations and communities must partner and build community outreach that entices and seeds young people of color, so they will know that there are opportunities in tech for them. Finally, corporations have got to find a way to PULL UP and support their key Black talent to help knock down the barriers to career development and management opportunities.

The system is made to screen out Blacks, not screen them in. The bottom line is that there is so much more work to be done, and it will take sponsorship, allyship and empathy to help increase our presence in technology. My vision for ten years from now is one where tech corporations have reached their new, higher goals buoyed by the momentum of the present boom. Only this time the Black and African American community is sharing in the prosperity, wealth and legacy that are part and parcel of high-tech careers.

EPILOGUE

My prayer for you is simply this. I pray God's best for you!

Father in the name of Jesus,

I come before You just thanking you for this day. I thank you for my fellow man and the person reading this book.

I pray for the young lady or man that is searching for their path Lord, and I pray that you strengthen and guide them.

I pray that they are able to use this book as a tool to see that You are always with them and that you will help guide them on the journey of their lives.

I pray that You are glorified in this example and that Your people will be able to see that You have made a way for them and that You have opened doors for them that no man can shut.

Lord, I pray that You use people to help hear our cry and to change the story for Black people in technology.

I pray that You heal people and this land. I pray this in Your son Jesus' name. Amen!

Revelations 12:11 kjv: *"And they overcame him by the blood of the Lamb, and by the word of their testimony; and they loved not their lives unto the death."*

RESOURCES

Here are some references I would like for you to take advantage of to help you in your journey toward tech:

1. A great program that introduces underrepresented people to technology: Job Training to Close the Opportunity Divide | Year Up
2. *Toastmasters* International: *Toastmasters* International -Home
3. Find yourself - Mentors, Sponsors & Coaches
4. Carla Harris Ted Talk on Sponsorship: Carla Harris: How to find the person who can help you get ahead at work | TED Talk
5. Your Body language shapes who you are – Amy Cuddy: Amy Cuddy: Your body language may shape who you are | TED Talk
6. Microsoft Learn for Microsoft Career Certifications: Microsoft Certifications | Microsoft Docs
7. Cisco Certifications: Certifications - Training & Certifications - Cisco
8. Program Management Certifications: Home | Scrum.org Project Management Institute | PMI
9. Emergenetics: Homepage - Emergenetics
10. Books
    a. Inclusion by Jennifer Brown

b. Strength Finders 2.0 by Tom Rath
c. What Got You Here Won't Get You There by Marshall GoldSmith

Everybody likes a good cheatsheat! Well, here's one for you. I call it the

Top 10 "shoulda's" I wish I had known when I was young like you:

1. Transferred to a college that was a better fit for me
2. Gained a degree; even an associates would have made my journey easier
3. Taken the chance to become a consultant sooner
4. Left my comfort zone, my hometown, for a bigger opportunity
5. Sought mentorship and sponsorship and invested in a career coach
6. Realized sooner that my intellect, unique brilliance, experiences, and skills were ultimately more powerful than a degree*
7. Done better self-care, personal training, and nutrition
8. Used my people skills to build a better network for career advancement
9. Not wasted time waiting for managers to do right by me
10. Utilized better self-promotion. Not confused selflessness with getting my opportunity. The corporation is not the church

* I know that points 2 and 6 seem to conflict. The fact of the matter is that with a degree, I would have had an easier journey, more options and more rapid access to advancement. However, at this point in my career, having industry experience, technical acumen, a work ethic, and a willingness to be a continuous learner, has outpaced my need for a degree.

ABOUT THE AUTHOR

Dwight Jones is a first-time author writing A *Black Journey in Tech* in about 30 days. He continues to be a champion for the African American and Black (AAB) community as a co-chair for the Microsoft Digital Blacks at Microsoft (BAM) employee resource group. In addition to publishing this memoir, Dwight continues to meet with the local community, schools, leaders, and teams within Microsoft to not only share the impact of Blacks to technology but also to drive awareness and action to help close the digital divide. Dwight also continues to stretch, learn, and grow his technical and leadership skills as a lead Program Manager supporting Microsoft's Government Cloud presence. Where he helps drive improvements into Microsoft products and services on behalf of the employee & customer experience. In February 2022 Dwight received the *Employee Experience Luminary Award*. This top award for the organization, is a testament to what we can achieve for cross-team impact at Microsoft. Dwight received this award for his work with Skype for Business & Microsoft Teams.

www.ingramcontent.com/pod-product-compliance
Lightning Source LLC
LaVergne TN
LVHW020413070526
838199LV00054B/3595